100

The Arts of Shinto

EDITORIAL SUPERVISION
FOR THE SERIES

Tokyo National Museum
Kyoto National Museum
Nara National Museum
with the cooperation of the
Agency for Cultural Affairs of
the Japanese Government

FOR THE ENGLISH VERSIONS

Supervising Editor
John M. Rosenfield
Department of Fine Arts, Harvard University
General Editor
Louise Allison Cort
Fogg Art Museum, Harvard University

THE ARTS OF SHINTO

by Haruki Kageyama

translated and adapted with an introduction by Christine Guth

New York • WEATHERHILL/SHIBUNDO • *Tokyo*

This book appeared originally in Japanese under the title Shintō Bijutsu *(Shintō Arts) as Volume 18 in the series Nihon no Bijutsu (Arts of Japan), published by Shibundō, Tokyo, 1967.*

The English text is based directly on the Japanese original, though some small adaptations have been made in the interest of greater clarity for the Western reader. Modern Japanese names are given in Western style (surname last), while premodern names follow the Japanese style (surname first).

For a list of the volumes in the series, see the end of the book.

First edition, 1973

Published jointly by John Weatherhill, Inc., 149 Madison Avenue, New York, N.Y. 10016, with editorial offices at 7-6-13 Roppongi, Minato-ku, Tokyo; and Shibundō, 27 Haraikata-machi, Shinjuku-ku, Tokyo. Copyright © 1967, 1973 by Shibundō; all rights reserved. Printed in Japan.

Library of Congress Cataloging in Publication Data: Guth, Christine. / The arts of Shinto. / (Arts of Japan, 4) / Adapted from Shinto bijutsu. / Bibliography: p. / 1. Art, Shinto. I. Kageyama, Haruki, 1916–   Shinto bijutsu. II. Title. / N8194. G8713 1973 / 704.948′9′9561 / 73–9640 / ISBN 0-8348-2706-9 ISBN 0-8348-2707-7 (pbk.)

Contents

Translator's Preface

ALTHOUGH ART FORMS associated with Shintō appear in general works on Japanese art history, the arts of Shintō have only recently become a separate field for research. Mr. Kageyama's study, which may be the first on the subject to appear in English, guides the reader through the complexities of Shintō art by treating it in its religious rather than its art historical context. There is little stress on stylistic and technical development or problems of chronology and connoisseurship; even approximate dating for some of the works illustrated is not provided. Such an approach is relevant in a country where, despite increasing materialism and technology, religious images on display in museums or galleries still inspire viewers to utter a brief prayer and make small offerings. In fact, religious symbolism overrides artistic considerations (including that of conservation) to such a degree that often shrine priests themselves have never seen the treasures preserved in their sanctuaries; much less can they be induced to show them to visitors. Mr. Kageyama has been faithful to this level of conviction, and I have attempted not to violate the flavor of the original.

Since Shintō, generally considered the indigenous and national religion of the Japanese people, is close to the hearts of the readers for whom this book was intended, many religious and historical terms required no explanation. The name "Kasuga Shrine" for instance, was sufficient to bring to mind the huge park in Nara through which deer wander freely, a place almost every Japanese child has visited during a spring school excursion. This cannot be true for Western readers, and in adapting this book I have reorganized certain sections and made numerous additions and deletions. Whenever possible, I replaced the parts eliminated with background material intended to contribute to an understanding of Shintō art within the broad cultural context already familiar to the Japanese audience. Needless to say, I am responsible for any errors in this adaption.

Although some of the technical terminology used in the Japanese version has been eliminated or simplified, I have retained a number of Japanese words that cannot be translated adequately into English without lengthy paraphrases. A brief definition of all such terms, however, can be found in the Glossary. Because a character can often be read in several ways, transcribing the names of deities, temples, or places is often problematic. This is especially true of names related to Shintō, which some scholars prefer to read in Japanese fashion and others in the Chinese-based pronunciation. Such is the case, for example, with the words for Imperial Regalia, read *mikusa no kandakara* in the former manner and *sanshū no shinki* in the latter. When both readings are commonly encountered, I have supplied both.

I would like to thank Professor Edwin Cranston of Harvard University for providing the translations of the poems in Chapters 3 and 4 as well as the one by the monk Saigyō in Chapter 8. It must be noted, however, that the latter poem given here is the one from the collected works of Saigyō rather than that quoted in the *Saigyō Monogatari Emaki*. My gratitude is also due to Professor John Rosenfield of Harvard University and Louise Cort, Assistant Curator of the Oriental Department of the Fogg Art Museum, whose aid and encouragement have been indispensable to the completion of this translation.

C. G.

Introduction

THE SHINTO CULT today encompasses individual and family, regional and national devotion; its combination of traditions, beliefs, and attitudes is one key to the Japanese character and principal social values. Association with this ancient cult begins very early in life. About thirty days after birth, a Japanese child is taken to a Shintō shrine and presented to its deities. He is then an *ujiko* or child of the deity of that locality, a parishioner of a particular shrine whose *kami* (deity) will be his special guardian throughout life. The term is also indicative of the enduring parent-child-like relationship that exists between the individual and the gods. Japanese visit their parish shrine to inform the gods of the transition from babyhood to childhood, to be married in the presence of the *kami,* or simply to pray or offer gratitude to them for recovery from an illness or success in an examination. The association does not end when they move to another locality, for they always remain parishioners of the same shrine and devotees of the same *ujigami.* This word, which originally designated the god worshiped by a particular clan, often its deified ancestor, has also come to mean the protector or tutelary deity of a certain area and those who dwell there. The residents of a specific locality—a region, village, or district within a city—are responsible for the upkeep of their *ujigami's* shrine and for presenting offerings to ensure his continued benevolence and spiritual vitality. They also participate in the festival during which the *kami* is borne throughout the area in a portable shrine or *mikoshi*—the occasion of a gay, often riotous procession. All those devoted to the same *ujigami* derive a feeling of solidarity and community identity from this bond. On a grander and more structured scale, the national unity of the Japanese people stems from a similar relationship with the principal deity of the Shintō pantheon, Amaterasu Omikami, also the ancestress of the imperial family, who is enshrined in Ise Shrine. This aspect of the Shintō faith has merited its being called the "national religion of Japan."

The object of Shintō worship is the *kami,* a concept perhaps better understood by the sensibilities than by definition. Some *kami,* such as deified ancestors, heroes, or the personified powers of nature, roughly correspond to the term "deity" or "god." Yet the vital force within anything is also a *kami.* It is not surprising, then, that the kimono, for instance, is made from uncut squares of fabric, or that paper-folding—*origami*—is such a highly developed popular art. Cutting fabric or paper destroys its divine spirit and is consequently avoided. The all-embracing and indefinable nature of the *kami* has been expressed in a poem perhaps composed by Saigyō or by the Heian-period Buddhist monk Gyōkyō, as quoted by Prince Takahito Mikasa in his address to the IXth International Congress for the History of Religions:

Unknown to me what resideth here
Tears flow from a sense of unworthiness and gratitude

Symbol of the kinship between man and the *kami* and consequently the center of Shintō worship on all levels is the shrine or *jinja*. Structures of varying sizes, often vermilion in color, they are generally approached by winding paths marked by stone lanterns and one or more pillared gates called *torii*. The shrine is a place of worship, but it is also a place for spiritual refreshment, surrounded as it is by a sacred park that evokes the close relationship to the natural environment that lies at the heart of the Shintō religion. Private worship is performed outside the shrine building. The devotee stands before the sanctuary, pulls a bell to get the deities' attention, claps his hands, utters a brief prayer, and then presents an offering—a few coins or perhaps glutinous rice cakes known as *mochi* or rice wine (*sakè*). Shintō rites are primarily expressions of thanks or gratitude to the deities whose benevolence and grace ensures the harmony of the universe. Although this creed might be said not to have a moral code, it does seem to have an underlying morality that consists in maintaining this harmony by spiritual and physical purity. The concept of evil therefore exists primarily in the form of impurity. This notion is reflected in many phases of Japanese life today, most obviously in the importance given to cleanliness. Even in a sport such as *sumō* wrestling, opponents continually throw salt into the ring to ensure its purity.

The primitive religion of the Japanese people, like that of most prehistoric peoples throughout the world, was shaped by the universal need to adjust to and explain the seasons and the great forces of nature. This orientation was especially important to the early clans of the Yamato plains south of Nara—the historic cradle of the Japanese nation—who lived by cultivating rice and fishing. Subject to the vagaries of climate, they regarded the world about them as awesome and mysterious. A river, for example, whose proper flow determined their very existence, seemed endowed with a superior power, a numinous nature that became the basis for its deification. Prayers and expressions of gratitude were consequently addressed directly to nature, and neither symbolic repositories of the divine spirit nor places to house them were necessary. However, archeological finds in the fourth- and fifth-century mounded tombs characteristic of the Tumulus or Kofun period as well as references in Shintō mythology indicate that objects such as mirrors, swords, and jewels, which perhaps initially had heirloom value, were thought to embody the divine essence of a *kami*. The belief that the numinous power of a deity might be captured and contained within an object which was then endowed with overwhelming spiritual energy was one of the primary factors leading to the creation of shrines, often on the natural sites previously set apart for ritual purposes. Later this concept evolved into the creation of devotional imagery.

Confucianist, Taoist, and perhaps Buddhist ideologies came into Japan during the fourth and fifth centuries and influenced Shintō to a certain degree, but it was not until the sixth century that the full impact of Indian Buddhism, which had wrought resounding spiritual and cultural changes throughout Asia, was felt in Japan. It brought with it the concept of the brevity and misery of life, the escape from which was the principal goal of the Buddhist adherent. Its contrasted markedly with the affirmation of life that lay at the heart of the indigenous religion. The Indian doctrine was also equipped with elaborate rituals, a well-organized monastic order, and a highly developed written and artistic tradition, all of which the Shintō of the time lacked. Moreover, it was characterized by a surprising capacity to adapt to local conditions—indeed, by the time it reached Japan, it had incorporated cults from India, Central Asia, and China within its sphere.

Had Buddhism not brought with it the highly advanced cultural achievements of India and China, it might not have found such ready acceptance among the Japanese aristocracy and intelligentsia who were its first adepts. Its advent led to the adoption of a writing system and governmental structure inspired by Chinese models, as well as to the development of monumental architecture, sculpture, and painting. Thus it was not until the eighth century that the legends and events that form the spiritual and historical background of the Shintō tradition were recorded in writing.

The two major extant records are the *Kojiki* (Record of Ancient Matters) and *Nihon Shoki* (Chronicles of Japan). They describe with slight variations the origins of the universe, the birth of the gods, and the peopling of the world, but these sections are followed by semihistorical chronologies of the imperial reigns through the seventh century. Consequently, although often called Shintō scriptures, this body of texts is quite different in nature from the Bible, the Koran, or other religious literature; in fact, it is Japan's oldest indigenous history.

The mythology of these compilations is both a cosmology and a dramatic personification of the forces of nature. It presents a universe divided into three worlds: the Heavenly Plain inhabited by the gods (Takamagahara), the manifest world with which the gods are in constant contact, and the underworld. It is a tripartite organization not unlike the ancient Greek universe. The creation of the world is attributed to two divine beings, who may be the personifications of the sky and the earth. These deities are also the parents of many of the principal gods of the Shintō pantheon—most notably Amaterasu Omikami, the sun goddess who rules Takamagahara, and the tempestuous Susano-o no Mikoto, who became the ruler of the underworld. Of all the powers of nature, the sun goddess became the most prominent as the special object of imperial and later national worship. However, Susano-o no Mikoto's role, in what might be considered the keystone of Japanese mythology, is not negligible. Once when he visited his sister Amaterasu Omikami in Takamagahara, he behaved so abominably that she retired into a cave, leaving the world in darkness. Subsequently, the other heavenly deities assembled to decide the best manner of enticing her out of this retreat, and the various means they chose—prayers; dances; hanging a mirror, jewels, and paper offerings on a sacred *sakaki* tree—are the mythological basis for many Shintō rituals.

The historical portions of these two documents describe the early history of Japan beginning with the descent to earth of Ninigi no Mikoto, Amaterasu Omikami's grandson and the ancestor of a line of emperors unbroken since Jimmu. It was to him that she gave the mirror embodying her spirit today enshrined in Ise; this same mirror is one of the three symbols of imperial rule. The legitimacy of the imperial line, the lineage of numerous important clans as well as their position within the social structure, and the groundwork for various clan and regional cults and beliefs was thus established. Basically, however, the texts glorify the imperial or Yamato clan and record the spread of its power throughout Japan.

Buddhism gradually became the dominant religion of Japan, but accommodated the native cult by erecting shrines within its temple compounds to provide protection by local *kami*. Similarly, there emerged the belief that *kami* were incarnations or manifestations of Buddhist gods. This led to the pairing of Shintō and Buddhist deities—at first only the most prominent, such as Amaterasu Omikami and the supreme being of the Buddhist pantheon, Dainichi Nyorai—but by the twelfth and thirteenth centuries, almost every deity in the Shintō pantheon was included. The elaborate concept providing each *kami* with a specific Buddhist counterpart is called the *honji-suijaku* theory; *honji*, which means "fundamental" or "root," refers to the Buddhist divinity, while *suijaku*, which means "trace" or "emanation," indicates the Shintō *kami*.

Shintō painting and sculpture, tinged by Buddhist stylistic and theological traits, is primarily comprised of works illustrating the correspondences of, for instance, the deified Nachi waterfall and the Buddhist form of Kannon, a compassionate deity believed to help man attain salvation. There is, however, a small body of sculptures, which although undoubtedly influenced by contemporary Buddhist work, convey a sense of spirituality quite distinct from that of Buddhist imagery. The massive, austere statues in the Matsuno-o Taisha in Kyoto, in particular, seem to retain the natural strength and solidity inherent in the tree trunk from which they were carved, and thus express a more native sensibility.

Buddhist and Shintō amalgamation reached a peak during the Kamakura and Muromachi periods (1185–1568), when the majority of the works discussed in this book were produced. Within Shintō circles, however, resistance to the wholesale absorption of national traditions by a foreign religion and culture grew until in 1868, at the beginning of a new political era in which the power previously held by a military government was returned to the imperial family, Buddhism and Shintō were officially separated in an attempt to purify the latter and reinforce the emperor's divine right to rule. As a result, all shrines were placed directly under government control and Buddhist images held by them were either destroyed or given to temples. But the numerous popular cults of deities whose strength lay in their fusion of both religions, such as that of the goddess of literature and music, Benzai-ten, were not undermined, and they still constitute a strong undercurrent in Japanese religion. The fact that most Japanese are associated with both a Buddhist temple and a Shintō shrine—often adjacent—is further evidence that this intermingling of faiths still comprises a vital part of Japanese life.

The Arts of Shinto

1

The Varieties of Shintō Art

Until recently, there have been no penetrating studies or comprehensive surveys of Shintō art as a form of expression in its own right. In fact, it has generally been considered a category of Buddhist art and as such has often been given the name *"suijaku bijutsu,"* which might be translated literally as "art depicting Shintō gods as subsidiary forms of Buddhist divinities," or *"shūgō bijutsu,"* a term labeling Shintō arts as no more than syncretic forms. It is true that the introduction of Buddhist culture was a strong stimulus for the portrayal of Shintō deities in human form and provided stylistic and technical models for Shintō artists; yet Shintō painting and especially sculpture nevertheless display unique characteristics and merit study in their own right. Shintō of course had forms of expression in the plastic arts before the coming of Buddhism, but the artistic tradition of the local cults and folk beliefs

of the fourth to seventh centuries, although rich, is perhaps more appropriately the domain of the archeologist. We shall therefore focus here on the art forms that developed between the eighth and the nineteenth centuries, when Shintō and Buddhism were part of a single broad cultural phenomenon.

Sculpture

The possibility of using wooden images of Shintō deities as objects of devotion first arose when shrines were established in places where natural phenomena had previously been worshiped. The development of such sculpture, particularly in the early Heian period (794–897), was conditioned by Esoteric Buddhism, whose doctrines provided for the easy assimilation of new deities into its pantheon and whose emphasis on

1.   Female deity. Painted wood; ht 50 cm. Fujiwara period.
Ozu Shrine, Shiga Prefecture.

2.   Female deity. Detail of Plate 1.

3.   Uda Mikumari Shrine. Surrounded by dense forest, this Mikumari jinja enshrines three kami of water in separate buildings placed ▷
side by side. This particular shrine was built in the fourteenth century in the Kasuga style (see Plate 77). The sunlight filtering through
the trees and the way in which the shrines seem almost enclosed by shrubbery convey visually that deep association between man, gods,
and nature that is the core of the Shintō religion. Nara Prefecture.

4. *Pair of male deities. Kasuga Shrine, Shiga Prefecture.*

the use of images for worship and meditation gave direction and shape to the arts. The Tendai and Shingon sects were the two principal Esoteric schools in Japan, and their art was the strongest stimulus in the ninth and tenth centuries. They fostered the gradual systemization of the relationship between Shintō and Buddhism, and so encouraged the inclusion of foreign deities in the range of subjects of Shintō art.

The oldest recorded Shintō sculpture is probably the one mentioned in the *Tado Jingū-ji Garan Engi Shizaichō* (Legends of Tado Jingū-ji) in 763. The deity named in this valuable document in the possession of the Tado Shrine in Mie Prefecture was originally the tutelary god of Mount Tado but came to be worshiped in the guise of a Bodhisattva—Tado-hōshuku Daibosatsu. The earliest extant examples of Shintō sculpture,

however, date only from the Jōgan era (859–77), when there was a marked predeliction among Buddhist sculptors for massive, solid images of wood with deeply carved waves of drapery and solemn facial expressions. This style and technique are reflected in the figures in the Matsuno-o Shrine in Kyoto (Plates 10, 46, 52) and to a certain extent in the Hachiman triad in the Yakushi-ji in Nara (Plates 41, 42) and the Tō-ji in Kyoto (Plates 43, 47, 48).

The attempt to express the characteristics peculiar to Shintō gave birth to a unique and independent sculptural form that reached its peak in the Late Heian or Fujiwara era (897–1185). The Buddhist sculpture of the time was gradually breaking away from the overwhelming influence of Esoterism, whose iconographic complexity and ferocious deities did not elicit the sym-

5. *Sumō wrestlers. Mikami Shrine, Shiga Prefecture.*

pathy or understanding of the masses. Instead there emerged a more appealing and understandable imagery reflecting the concepts of the new mass-oriented religions promising salvation to all.

Shintō sculpture of this period, however, relatively detached from Buddhist trends, came to be strongly influenced by the pomp and splendor of the imperial court. Shrines were modeled after palaces, deities were regarded as princes and princesses, and religious ceremonies were deeply permeated by court practices. Images of male deities were garbed in formal court dress like men of rank (Plate 98), and female deities in the five-layer T'ang-style robes then popular among ladies, exemplified by the portrayal of Niu Myōjin in Plate 74. Shrines were often equipped with curtained daises similar to the "curtains of state" behind which

lords and ladies of rank received visitors. The origins of the present-day *mikoshi* or portable shrine (Plate 31), used on festive occasions to transport the deities, can be traced to the use of imperial carriages as vehicles of the gods. Even religious festivals and rituals reflected the changes in this direction. The lovely princesslike figure of the goddess Tamayori-hime (Plates 55 and 56), for example, epitomizes this rapprochement between the court and Shintō.

Shintō sculpture tends to be very conservative. In early Heian times, both Shintō and Buddhist sculptors used the single-woodblock or *ichiboku-zukuri* technique, but the latter subsequently abandoned it for the joined-woodblock or *yosegi-zukuri* technique, since figures made in this manner were less apt to crack and were easier to produce in great numbers. And although

正一位勲三等若狭彦大明神

6. Legends of the Wakasa-hiko Shrine, Wakasa Province. *Detail of a handscroll. This scroll relates the history of Wakasa-hiko and Wakasa-hime, tutelary deities of Wakasa Province in present-day Fukui Prefecture, along with that of the family of attendant priests. The portion reproduced here depicts Kasa no Ason Setsubun, the ancestor of the hereditary priests of the shrine, as an old man paying obeisance at the shrine. Kamakura period. Kyoto National Museum.*

7. Diagram of Gion Shrine. *This somewhat schematic record of the layout and appearance of the principal sanctuary, subordinate shrines, pagoda, and honji-dō of the Gion Shrine was probably produced some time after their reconstruction following a fire in 1221. The work may also, however, have been used for devotional purposes as a sort of* mandala. *According to the inscription on the back, it was painted in 1330 by a certain Ryūen, a member of the Gion Shrine painting atelier. Yasaka Shrine, Kyoto.* ▷

8. *Kōya and Niu. Drawing of the two tutelary deities of Mount Kōya. 1335. Shirayama-hime Shrine, Ishikawa Prefecture.*

examples of Shintō sculpture made from a single piece of wood, occasionally with appendages such as hands and feet added from separate pieces, are common well into the Kamakura period (1185–1336), there are some images that belie this general statement. Among them is the renowned sculpture of Hachiman in the guise of a monk (Plate 57) by Kaikei, one of the foremost Buddhist sculptors of the thirteenth century. Its highly developed realism, portraitlike features, and joined-woodblock technique are characteristic of Buddhist imagery of the Kamakura period.

One fundamental point to be kept in mind when considering Shintō sculpture is that, unlike Buddhist imagery, it was not made to be seen by devotees. Except for the Esoteric sects, Buddhist images were placed in halls where devotees might contemplate them and find comfort in their benevolent appearance or be struck with awe by their ferocity. In other words, visual effect contributed to the heightening of the viewer's feeling of religious mystery and determined the artist's approach. Shintō sculptures, on the other hand, were placed in portable shrine boxes behind curtains in special parts of a shrine. Intentionally hidden from view, images came to be revered symbolically in the minds of devotees. This means of intensifying the sense of religious awe and mystery is similar to the effect achieved by the "secret images" of Esoteric Buddhist sects, and may in fact have been influenced by Esoteric practice. There is therefore a fundamental disparity between the creative consciousness of the Japanese artists who made Shintō and Buddhist sculptures.

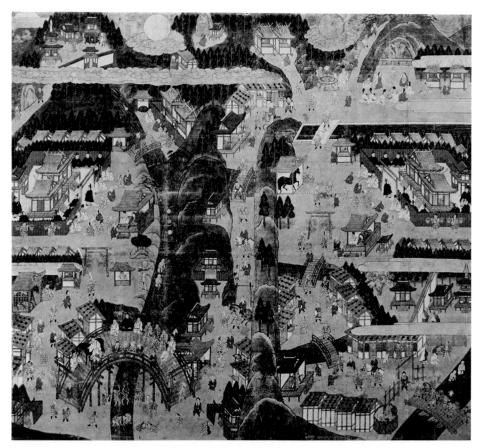

9. Ise Shrine Pilgrimage Mandala. *Colors on silk; ht 100 cm, w 181 cm. Ise Shrine Administration Agency, Mie Prefecture.*

Painting

•MANDALAS. Portrayals of *kami*, with or without their Buddhist counterparts, hold a key position in Shintō painting and have consequently been the primary object of research on the part of art historians. Through them one can reach some understanding of Shintō iconography and thus better determine the role of a deity in a particular cult and his identity in another context or medium. Images are often arranged in the form of a *mandala*—in the strict sense, a systematic diagram in which the position of each deity in the universe and his relationship to others is established. Of Buddhist origin, this pictorial concept came to be interpreted rather broadly in Japan so that paintings of a single deity or even scenes of shrine activities were

also referred to as *mandalas*. Although the aim of a *mandala* depicting a group of deities was partly didactic, it also tried to capture the likeness of a *kami* as he appeared in a dream or vision or as he was traditionally thought to look. Since *mandalas* were made primarily as offerings for the temple tutelary deities or for the Buddhist *honji* (Buddhist counterpart of the Shintō *kami*) and for use in important religious ceremonies, they exist in numerous varieties. Among the most renowned are those produced at the Kasuga Shrine in Nara and the shrines at Kumano and on Mount Hiei, and for the cult of the god Hachiman.

•EMAKI. The long picture scroll or *emaki* format was put to good use by Shintō artists in order to illustrate legends *(engi)* or miracle stories *(reigen)* associated with

11.   Mandala of Mount Fuji. *Colors on silk; ht 91.5 cm, w 67.3 cm. Late Muromachi period. Fuji Hongū Sengen Shrine, Shizuoka Prefecture.*

12.   *Michizane protesting to Heaven of his false accusation. Section of the fifth scroll of the* Kitano Tenjin Engi. *Kamakura period, 13th century. Kitano Temman Shrine, Kyoto.*

◁   10.   Female deity (himegami). *Detail. Painted wood; ht 87 cm. This sculpture reflects the reverence toward women that constituted an archetypal part of primitive and prehistoric beliefs in both East and West. The matronly female images in clay of the Jōmon period in Japan were followed, with the development of* haniwa *in the Tumulus period, by portrayals of shamanesses; later in shrine Shintō, due partly to the influence of Buddhism, wooden images were created, and in the figure from the Matsuno-o Shrine, both the mystery of Shintō expression and the dignified composure of Esoteric Buddhism can be discerned. Mid-ninth century. Matsuno-o Shrine, Kyoto.*

13. *The Izumishima Shrine. Detail of the* Ippen Shōnin Eden *(Pictorial Biography of the Monk Ippen), by En'i Hōgen. Long handscroll on silk. 1299. Kankikō-ji, Kyoto.*

14. Nenjū Gyōji Emaki *(Annual Rites and Ceremonies). Detail. Edo period, 17th century. Tanaka Collection, Tokyo.*

15. Omatsuri no yama *(festival procession of floats in the shape of mountains). Detail of the* Sairei Ezōshi *(Scroll of Festival Scenes).* Muromachi period. Maeda Foundation, Tokyo.

kami or shrines, or to depict the adventures of Buddhist monks who fostered Shintō beliefs and ideas. Illustrating the legends of the god of the Kitano Shrine in Kyoto is the *Kitano Tenjin Engi* (Legends of Kitano Tenjin Shrine), one of the foremost examples in this genre. The narrative evolved from a series of tales that were transmitted first orally, then in writing, and later illustrated.

The strange and terrible story of Kitano Tenjin begins with the birth of Sugawara Michizane (845–903), who was to become a powerful imperial minister. Although innocent of any crime, he was maligned by a rival and sent into exile, where he died. The scene illustrated in Plate 12 is from the section of the scroll depicting his exile in Kyūshū when he climbed atop a mountain and proclaimed the injustice of his punishment to the gods. Following his death, the tale tells of his deification with the title of Temma Daijizai

Tenjin and the subsequent construction of a shrine in the Kitano district in Kyoto according to instructions transmitted through an oracle. The shrine was built in order to pacify the angry spirit of Michizane, which according to the beliefs of the time would avenge itself for his mistreatment.

The *Kasuga Gongen Reigen Ki* (The Kasuga Gongen Miracles), discussed in Chapter 5, is an example of narrative scrolls that illustrate a collection of tales of miraculous events—in this case fifty-six stories about the deities of the Kasuga cult. Another example of Shintō illustrated narrative scrolls is the *Sannō Rishō Ki* (Miraculous Stories about the God Sannō), which focuses on the events surrounding the tutelary deity of Mount Hiei and, since this mountain is the center of the Tendai sect, also relates many of the activities of the Buddhist monks there. In fact, the work is so rich in Buddhist flavor that it is also commonly called

16.   Screen of the Chikubu Island Festival. *Edo period. Yamato Bunkakan, Nara.*

the *Sammon Sōden* (Biographies of Monks on Mount Hiei). *Kakemono* (hanging scrolls) of shrines or of mass pilgrimages were also executed to accompany oral narratives about a particular cult. The *Kumano Nachi Shrine Pilgrimage Mandala* (Plate 131), *mandala* of the two Ise Shrines (Plate 9), and Fuji *mandala* (Plate 11) are all examples of this type.

Since the lines between Buddhism and Shintō were not very clear, particularly during the period when the majority of the *emaki* discussed here were painted, it is not surprising that picture scrolls about Buddhist temples or monks' lives may also be considered to be Shintō painting. In fact, many devout Buddhist monks were drawn by the appeal of the native deities, whose worship formed a strong undercurrent in the religious life of the times. Ippen Shōnin (1239–89), for example,

was a wandering missionary concerned with the spiritual welfare of the masses. He was a devotee of Amida, the Buddha of the West, who would descend to welcome the souls of believers and carry them back to his paradise. Yet Ippen's pictorial biography, the *Ippen Shōnin Eden* (Pictorial Biography of the Monk Ippen), painted in a twelve-scroll *emaki* in 1299, includes many realistic illustrations of the Shintō establishments he visited, such as the Iwashimizu (Plate 104), Izumishima (Plate 13), and the Kumano shrines (Plate 127), and is a valuable document for the study of shrine architecture and layout in the Kamakura period. The early thirteenth-century *Saigyō Monogatari Emaki* (Biography of the Monk Saigyō) is also precious for historians, and its portrayal of Saigyō's pilgrimage to Kumano, shown in Plate 125, is among the most sensitive and

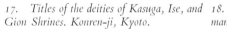

17. *Titles of the deities of Kasuga, Ise, and Gion Shrines. Konren-ji, Kyoto.*

18. *Titles of the deities of Hachiman, Kumano, and Kitano Tenjin Shrines. Konren-ji, Kyoto.*

19. *Portrait of Emperor Godaigo with titles of deities. 1399. Seijōkō-ji, Kanagawa Prefecture.*

evocative illustrations of the religious fervor of the time.

Like many religious festivals throughout the world, Shintō festivals are generally gay, even riotous occasions of public enjoyment and entertainment, whose cultic nature is often obscured. Their origin might lie in the desire to offer thanks to the gods for an abundant harvest, to present them with the first fruits, or to gain their protection against evil, which often took the form of impurity. They generally consist of elaborate and colorful processions in which the public participates by helping to carry the *mikoshi*, the portable shrine in which the *kami* is temporarily housed while he visits the shrine precincts and the village or town whose special guardian he is. These *matsuri*, as they are called, capture the enthusiasm and spirit of devotees

of a shrine and have consequently often been recorded by artists. Plates 14 and 15 impart the lively mood of various *matsuri*. The former is a section from the *Nenjū Gyōji Emaki* (Annual Rites and Ceremonies), the original of which was executed in the late Heian period, perhaps at the request of Emperor Goshirakawa (r. 1155–58). A precious source of information about twelfth-century ceremonies at the imperial court, as well as those at shrines and temples, it also gives detailed glimpses of plebeian life in Kyoto. (The original has been lost, and extant versions are all copies from the eighteenth century or later.)

·PICTORIAL RECORDS. The periodic reconstruction of a shrine and renewal of its treasures *(shikinen sengū)* was of considerable religious significance. The requirement

20. *Kanō Sanraku: Votive Picture of a Horse* (Ema). *Momoyama period. Kaizu Tenjin Shrine, Shiga Prefecture.*

that shrines be rebuilt or repaired without any modi-
fications over the years motivated the production of
another type of Shintō painting, sometimes best described as landscape, but often closer to architectural
sketches, for they indicate with utmost accuracy shrine
structures, their layout, and the boundaries of the
shrine compound. Though often used as devotional
paintings, they must also have served as records. As
works of art, many have an appealing simplicity and
charm. A case in point is the *Sannō Shrine Mandala*
reproduced in Plate 123; although a devotional work,
it nevertheless furnishes indispensable data concerning
the shrine as it appeared in the Kamakura period. The
careful design in the *Gion Shrine Plan* (Plate 7) and
its coloring and style suggest that its creator had
both documentary and decorative aims. The *Chikubu*

Island Festival painting (Plate 16) has a similar aesthetic appeal.

Illustrations of shrine treasures and artifacts were
often the subject of scrolls kept as records, and the Imperial Household Library today has some twenty examples of scrolls depicting sacred treasures. The names
of all such scrolls and drawings throughout the country are recorded in the *Kōko Gafu* (Chronicles of Ancient Art), a late nineteenth-century work that gives
us valuable clues into the history of shrine restorations
and reconstructions, and often provides evidence of a
more general historical nature.

•CALLIGRAPHY. Fine calligraphy has always been highly
prized in Japan, and examples of calligraphy by emperors and renowned monks, or even the names of

21. Ise Ryōgū Shimpō Zukan *(Scroll Illustrating Treasures of the Two Ise Shrines). Detail depicting sculpture of a horse with horse trappings. Maeda Foundation, Tokyo.*

deities written by a good hand, were considered objects of veneration. Reverence for the titles of deities (Plates 17 and 18) may derive from the Buddhist practice of worshiping and meditating on single letters of symbolic value written in Sanskrit in Siddham script. In the Kamakura period, the titles of the deities Amaterasu Omikami, Hachiman Okami, and Kasuga Daimyōjin were especially popular (Plate 19). Through the influence of the Riron sect of Shintō in the Muromachi period (1336–1568), such devotional calligraphy was widely circulated as the object of a broad popular cult. Reproductions of titles by the hands of emperors, especially Gonara (r. 1526–57), Goyōzei (r. 1586–1611), and Reigen (r. 1663–87), were also widely diffused among the masses and in religious brotherhoods, since their production was simple and inexpensive.

•EMA. Shintō art also includes votive paintings called *ema,* which most commonly depict horses. It was an ancient Shintō custom to present the gods, particularly those of rain, with a black horse when rain was desired and with a white one when there was too much rain. Offering a horse meant giving a highly prized possession, since this animal played an important role in the everyday life of ancient society, especially in military affairs, agriculture, and transportation.

In time, however, live horses were replaced by paintings of black or white horses on wooden tablets, which came to be known as *ema.* The themes of these votive paintings were expanded to include specific images of wished-for objects or of shrine structures and festival scenes; *ema* were also made to express thanks for a wish fulfilled. They are therefore interesting from both the religious and artistic standpoints.

The *Shintō Myōmoku Ruijū,* an anonymous illustrated eighteenth-century document concerning Shintō customs and treasures, mentions *ema,* but the oldest references to them appear in a Heian collection of poetry called the *Honchō Monzui,* which describes the presentation of pictures of horses painted on paper

22. *Sculpture of a horse* (shimme). *Hyōzu Shrine, Shiga Prefecture.*

(today they are generally executed on wooden plaques) to the Kitano Shrine in Kyoto in 1012, and in the *Hoku-zan Shō*'s description of *ema* painted on boards given to the Tamukeyama Hachiman Shrine in 949. It would seem, therefore, that this practice developed at an early date.

The numbers of *ema* of high aesthetic quality in the Kyoto Kitano, Yasaka, and Inari shrines as well as the Itsukushima Shrine in Hiroshima Prefecture and the Kotohira Shrine in Kagawa Prefecture indicate their importance and popularity. Exemplary works of this type are the painted *ema* of the Yamauba (The Old Woman of the Mountains) by Rosetsu (1755–99) now in Itsukushima, the votive picture of a dove by Okyo (1733–95) in Iwashimizu, and the one of a horse by Kanō Motonobu (1476–1559) in the Kamo Shrine of

Hyōgo Prefecture. The plaque shown in Plate 20 was painted by Kanō Sanraku (1559–1635), a prominent member of the Kanō school of painting.

A considerable number of sculpted horses as well as ornamental horse trappings inspired by the same devotional purpose were also given to shrines. Of the former, there is a small pair in the Itsukushima Shrine and another in the Hyōzu Shrine in Shiga Prefecture (Plate 22). The Kasuga Shrine in Nara also has a collection of archery equipment used by horsemen. The section of a scroll illustrating treasures in the two Ise Shrines *(Ise Ryōgū Shimpō Zukan)* shown in Plate 21 is of particular interest, since it records data concerning the small sculpture of a horse depicted in the scroll; as might be expected, the figure was offered on the occasion of a shrine renewal.

2

Shrine Treasures

A great variety of ritual objects was produced in the distinctive religious environment of Shintō. These include objects of high solemnity offered for the use of the deities, such as daggers, bows and arrows, and sacred garments, as well as utensils of daily use and toilet cases. All such objects were renewed according to religious custom when a shrine was rebuilt and its deity transferred to a new one in the ceremony called *shikinen sengū*. *Shikinen sengū*, a concept peculiar to Shintō, is not merely the rebuilding of a structure and the replacing of its ritual implements; rather, it is the renewal of the very spiritual life of the *kami*.

The Imperial Regalia

The most prominent and also the most ancient Shin-

tō ritual and symbolic objects are mirrors, swords, and the curved jewels called *magatama*. Ancient literary references and excavations around early tombs and ritual sites give ample evidence of their importance. Plate 23, for example, shows a sixth-century *haniwa* sculpture of a woman wearing a necklace of *magatama* beads. The special reverence for these three types of objects seems to have evolved from their role as valued personal ornaments, ritual implements, and weapons in ancient society. In time, however, they came to be treasured as family heirlooms and hereditary symbols of power within a clan and were considered objects that endowed their owners with magico-religious powers. Later, with the emergence of the Yamato state, they became symbols of divine rulership and have been retained to this day as the Imperial Regalia, em-

23. Haniwa *clay sculpture, woman with necklace of* maga-tama *beads. Ht 28.9 cm. Kyoto University.*

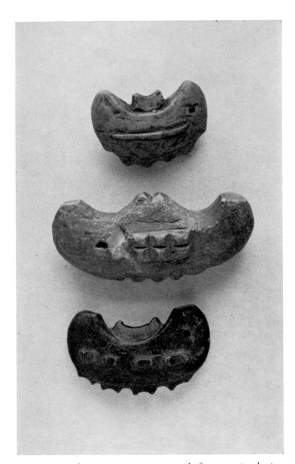

24. Komochi-magatama *excavated from a ritual site. Deguchi Collection, Kyoto.*

blems of the uninterrupted transmission of imperial authority from the legendary first emperor, Jimmu Tennō, to the present one.

Each of the three symbols that comprised the Imperial Regalia bears a name: the comma-shaped jewels are called Yasakani no Magatama, which indicates that they are elongated in shape and strung together; the sacred sword, Kusanagi no Tsurugi (Grass-quelling Sword); and the divine mirror either *naishi dokoro* or Yata no Kagami. The former name probably derives from the fact that a class of women attendants named *naishi* were in charge of the sacred mirror, while the latter refers to its shape, which is like that of an eight-petaled flower.

According to Shintō classics, whose accounts vary occasionally, the symbolic value of the three treasures

developed from the tradition that the god Ninigi no Mikoto brought them with him when he descended from Takamagahara (the Heavenly Plain) to rule the Central Land of the Reed Plains. Already during the age of the gods, however, a mirror and jewels played a considerable role in the quasi-ritual enticement of the goddess Amaterasu Omikami out of the cave into which she had retired, leaving the world in darkness.

Of the three, the mirror is of greatest importance, since it came to be considered the manifestation of Amaterasu, the ancestress of the imperial family. The fact that the Yata no Kagami embodies the *mitama* (soul or spirit) of this deity endowed it with over-whelming numinous power. For this reason, the emperor Sujin (r. 97–30? B.C.) transferred it from his palace, where it had been traditionally kept, to a spe-

25.   *Assorted jewels* (magatama) *excavated from a ritual site. Omiya no Me Shrine, Kyoto.*

cial shrine. Soon thereafter it was placed in the sanctuary devoted to Amaterasu Omikami at Ise, where it has remained to this day. Similarly, the sword was enshrined in the Atsuta Shrine in Nagoya, and only replicas of both divine implements are kept in the imperial palace. The jewels, however, seem to have been viewed in a different light—perhaps more like relics in the Catholic world, which do not need to be kept in a sacred place—and remain in the possession of the imperial family.

These traditional accounts concerning the transmission of the mirror and sword from the palace provide valuable clues to the reasons behind the construction of shrines, and even today, many sanctuaries preserve such objects as *goshintai,* or the material repository of the divine spirit of the deity. A number of shrines possess curiously shaped *magatama* with incrustations on their surface, like those shown in Plate 24. Called *komochi-magatama* or "child-bearing jewels," they are among the most unusual and little understood developments in the history of the three treasures. Although most classics speak of only three treasures, the *Kujiki* relates that Ninigi no Mikoto carried ten types of *kandakara* (divine implements) with him when he descended to rule Japan. The *Kujiki* also indicates that the names of the ten *kandakara* should be invoked in case of illness or misfortune, that waving them about will rid a place of illness, and that they are capable of restoring life. Numerous tales describe the *kandakara* as possessing supernatural powers, and the names of such deities as Ninigi no Mikoto, Tamayori-hime, and Kushi Akurutama no Mikoto, all of which include

26. *Clay pottery excavated from a ritual site in Nara Prefecture. Kyoto National Museum.*

the character meaning "jewel," may reflect the tradition that shamanistic mediums and members of families of divine rulers derived their special powers from possession of one of them.

Divine Treasures

With the lessening of the emphasis on nature in the Nara period (646–794) and the emergence of the concept that the shrine was a permanent abode where the deity was ever-present, distinct changes took place in the nature of Shintō rites and accessories, for the precepts of shrine Shintō *(shaden Shintō),* as the religion of the post-Nara period is called, specified that ceremonies be performed as if the deity were actually in attendance. Thus, food, clothing, articles of daily use, and furniture came to be considered essential for the deity's comfort. The items provided for such use are generally designated *shimpō,* or divine treasures, to distinguish their fundamentally different religious role from that of *shahō,* or shrine treasures.

As described earlier, it also became customary—even necessary from the religious standpoint—to renew the divine treasures whenever a shrine was rebuilt or repaired. And objects donated for the use of the *kami* of important shrines by the emperor of course had great religious value. Generally he gave offerings on the occasion of his enthronement in order to ensure the continuity of the power of the gods and their protection throughout his reign. The *Kōtai Jingū Gishikichō,* a

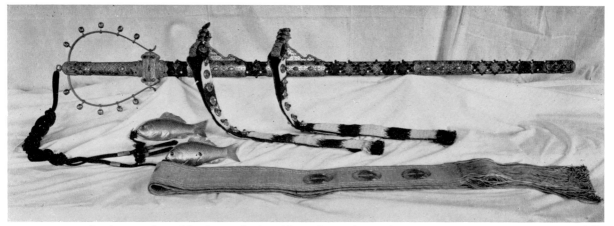

27. *Jewel-encrusted sword for the use of a deity* (shimpō). *Ise Shrine Administration Agency, Mie Prefecture.*

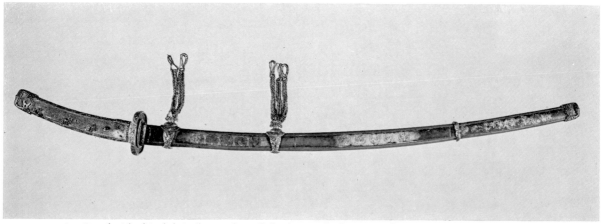

28. *Sword with plaited chain* (hyōgo kusari) *for the use of a deity. Kamakura period. Atsuta Shrine, Nagoya.*

valuable record compiled in the ninth century by officials of the Kōtai Shrine, the inner sanctuary of the Ise Shrine devoted to Amaterasu Omikami, indicates that the making of treasures when the shrine was rebuilt every twenty years (as is still the case today) was an observance of such consequence that the same degree of care and expense went into their renewal as into the rebuilding of the shrine itself.

The treasures include gold and silver *tatari* and *kasebi,* utensils whose exact significance is not known, long swords, a Japanese harp *(koto)* with ornamental ridge tiles, linen chests of gold and silver gilt, gold and silver gilt bells, a jewel-encrusted sword, bows made from catalpa wood, quivers made of brocade-covered cattail, leather, archer's armguards, and a halberd. Ten types of ceremonial garb are also named, and in both the Naikū (the inner sanctum) and the Gekū (the outer sanctum), as well as in the subordinate shrines of the Kōtai Jingū, these too had to be renewed. Because all these objects had to be made according to prescribed ancient models, many skills were preserved, and from this point of view, the offering of treasures to shrines is of considerable historical and artistic importance. Moreover, many such treasures have been preserved because of the custom of burying them within the shrine compound when the sanctuary was rebuilt.

Although noteworthy examples of lacquered boxes *(tebako),* sacred garments, and weapons and arms were donated to ordinary shrines, the Itsukushima, Kuma-

29. *Miniature arms for the use of a male deity. Fujiwara period. Itsukushima Shrine, Hiroshima Prefecture.*

no Hayatama, Tsurugaoka Hachiman, and Kasuga shrines are the greatest repositories of such objects, many of which have been designated National Treasures or Important Cultural Properties. Plate 27 shows a deity's jewel-encrusted sword, while Plate 28 shows one with chain-link pendants in the Nagoya Atsuta Shrine. The pendants of this particular type of sword, called *hyōgo kusari,* were plaited by artisans in the imperial armory, and the gold bands on the sheath decorated with a repoussé design are characteristic of the Kamakura period. The Hime Shrine in Fukui Prefecture and the Itsukushima Shrine possess similar *hyōgo kusari* swords of excellent quality. A gold plaque on the Atsuta sword bears an inscription indicating that it was offered in 1293 for the use of Ya-

tsurugi Myōjin, the tutelary deity of the Kasuga area today enshrined in the most important of the subordinate shrines in the Atsuta compound.

The Itsukushima Shrine is particularly rich in divine treasures of fine workmanship, some of which date from late Heian times (897–1185). Those depicted here include some of a group of miniature implements for male deities (Plate 29) said to have been Emperor Antoku's (r. 1180–83) toys. However, it is probable that their size was determined by that of the subordinate shrine for which they were made. Gifts of this type as well as clothes for the use of the *kami* are often considerably larger in size than those used by ordinary men, and examples in miniature are rather unusual. Those at Itsukushima seem to be of the Fuji-

30. *Lacquered toilet case with plum-tree design for the use of a female deity. Mishima Shrine, Shizuoka Prefecture.*

wara (late Heian) period, which is in accordance with the tradition that they were used by Emperor Antoku; as such, they are extremely precious records of court customs and of military practices. Since the items shown here are rather irregular in scale—for example, the wood scepter *(shaku)* is considerably larger than the other objects, and the arrows and quiver do not match—it is possible that a variety of pieces was gathered together to form a set. Although the arrows, sword, sheath, and hilt are all made of copper with hammered designs, they are skillful reproductions of the actual weapons of the time.

Among the items presented to female deities are the numerous lacquer boxes for cosmetics that provide valuable knowledge about lacquerwork from Heian to medieval times. The cosmetic cases preserved at the Kumano Shrine are particularly renowned, but there are numerous other fine examples, such as the one with a plum-tree design given by Taira no Masako to the Mishima Shrine (Plate 30), a Sumiyoshi lacquerwork box given to the goddess Nikkō Nyotai Gongen in 1229, and another with a chrysanthemum pattern given to the Atsuta Shrine by Ashikaga Yoshimasa (1435–90).

•MIKOSHI. Portable shrines, called *mikoshi* or *shin'yo,* are undoubtedly among the clearest indications of the influence of court practices on shrine culture, for although they are found today in shrines throughout the country and have come to be inseparable from the

31. *Portable shrine* (mikoshi). *Fujiwara period. Tomobuchi Hachiman Shrine, Wakayama Prefecture.*

Shintō festivals in which the masses actively participate, they are derived from the carriages used to transport noblemen of the court. The two principal types are distinguished by the emblem on the roof, either a phoenix *(hōren)* or a knoblike form *(sōkaren).* The carriages originated in China, and it is said that they were first used in Japan to transport the deity Hachiman from Usa to Tōdai-ji in Nara times. However, the custom does not seem to have gained widespread acceptance until the Heian period. The traditional shape of *mikoshi* in Japan was modeled after the four-cornered curtained platform used inside shrines, but hexagonal, octagonal, and even round ones also exist.

The oldest extant *mikoshi* is a gilt one presented to the Konda Hachiman Shrine in Kawachi by Mina-moto Yoritomo (1147–99), the first of the Minamoto shoguns, and today designated a National Treasure. Almost as old is the one in the Tomobuchi Hachiman Shrine on Kii Peninsula, also a National Treasure, which is reproduced in Plate 31. An ancient document reveals that it was originally made for the deities of the Iwashimizu Hachiman Shrine, but that in 1228 it was bestowed by imperial grant on the Tomobuchi Hachiman Shrine, a subordinate shrine of Iwashimizu, where it is one of the sacred palanquins still used to transport the *kami* from the principal shrine to a temporary dwelling at the foot of the mountain. The same document also indicates that at the time there was a knoblike emblem on the roof, so it would seem that the phoenix there now was added at a later date.

32. Kakebotoke *with the twelve Kumano Gongen* (honji) *in relief.*
Gilt copper; diam 41.3 cm. Kamakura period. Hosomi Collection.

Mishotai and Kakebotoke

The mirrors that have long been valued as objects of special religious and historical significance in Japan have been found in great numbers among the grave goods buried in tumuli during the Kofun period (250–552). Their manner of arrangement in tombs indicates that they were regarded as ornaments or utensils. But the presence of more than were necessary for the deceased's personal use suggests that they were also believed to have mysterious powers and were treasured as were swords and jewels. The origin of their use in early Shintō rites may derive from shamanesses' use of mirrors with bells in primitive rituals. This ancient popular concept is reflected even today in the presence of mirrors called *mishotai* enshrined as the material repository of the spirit of a *kami* in many shrines. Ancient documents refer to the creation of these objects by a guild of mirror makers and to the fact that the names of many shrines derive from those of mirrors enshrined within them.

The practice of worshiping mirrors inscribed with Buddhist images or Siddham characters emerged with the development of the Shintō-Buddhist amalgamation, and many mirrors of this type still exist today. By far the greatest number have been unearthed on Mount Kimpu (Omine-san) in Nara Prefecture, where the ascetic Shugendō sect originated, and most common among the discoveries are those depicting Zaō Gongen, the special guardian of that sect. Plate 34

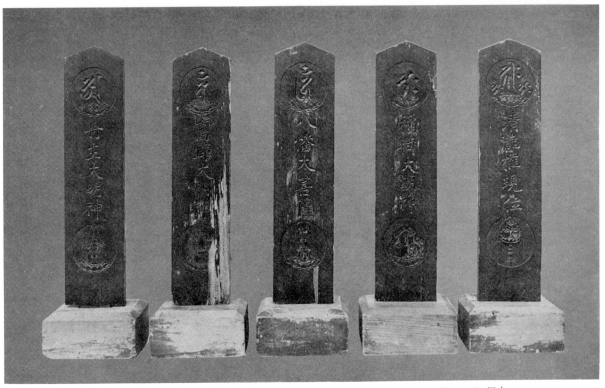

33. Wooden plaques symbolizing the five gongen of Kongō-ji. Ht 52 cm. 1341. Kongō-ji, Tokyo.

34. Mirror depicting Zaō Gongen. Copper; diam 20 cm. Late Heian period. Tokyo University of Arts.

35. Mirror inscribed with image of Nyoirin Kannon and the guardians of the four directions. Daigo-ji, Kyoto.

36. Image of deer bearing symbols of the five Kasuga Gongen. Ht 105.3 cm. Muromachi period. Hosomi Collection.

37. Relic pagoda used in the Kasuga cult. Copper and crystal; ht 17.3 cm. Kamakura period. Kōsetsu Collection.

shows one such mirror made in a flowerlike eight-lobed shape. Plate 35 shows a beautifully incised eight-petaled mirror with an image of the Nyoirin Kannon (the *honji* of Daigo-ji's Seiryū Gongen shown in Plate 69) placed under a baldachin and surrounded by the guardians of the four directions. As might be expected of a work of art produced in the Esoteric Buddhist atmosphere of the Daigo-ji temple, the figure is iconographically correct and its technical quality extremely high. Besides those with images, mirrors with Siddham letters representing the names of deities, with calligraphy, or with writing in red have also been discovered, but all are characteristic of the same type of belief.

The development of this genre led to the emergence

of circular metal plaques with one or more Buddhist figures called *kakebotoke*. The mature style of *kakebotoke* (Plate 32) took on a three-dimensional form due to the addition of cast Buddhist images attached to the copper plate. This particular *kakebotoke* is of the twelve Kumano Gongen (incarnations of the Shintō *kami* as Buddhist deities). Each figure is made of cast copper to which a mandorla (halo) made from another thin piece of copper has been added by inserting it into the round plaque; the whole is gilded, as are most *kakebotoke*.

During the Kamakura and Muromachi periods, as *kakebotoke* spread throughout the country with the ideas of *shimbutsu shūgō* (the fusion of *kami* and Buddhas, the intermingling of Shintō and Buddhism), the

38. *Embroidered banners. Hyōzu Shrine, Shiga Prefecture.*

custom of hanging them inside shrines became common. Moreover, *kakebotoke* were offered by devotees to a single shrine for memorial services, and as can be seen in the painting reproduced in Plate 123, they were hung both inside and outside the building. Many of these plaques were probably destroyed during the official separation of Shintō and Buddhism in the Meiji era, but even now quite a few can be found in country shrines. For example, two hundred and forty-seven still hang in the Nabi Shrine in Gifu Prefecture, which developed from primitive beliefs centered around Mount Kōga.

The simple oblong plaques that are the material repositories of the *mitama* of the five tutelary deities of the Kongō-ji at Nanao, Hino City, Tokyo appear in Plate 33. The subsidiary shrine of this temple was originally consecrated to Hachiman by Minamoto Yoritomo, but later Inari Daimyōjin, Seiryū Gongen, Kōya Daimyōjin, and Niu Daimyōjin—all well-known Shintō deities—were added. According to temple tradition, these long wooden plaques were made to replace decayed Shintō sculptures and *honji-butsu* originally kept in this shrine. On them appear the names of the five deities, those of their *honji* in both Chinese characters and Siddham letters, and their symbolic forms, as well as the date 1341.

Both Plate 36—a *goshintai* (material object in which the divine spirit resides) of a standing deer—and Plate 37—a reliquary pagoda supported by deer—were inspired by the Kasuga cult (see Chapter 5). Judging

39. Keman *with Siddham symbol of Dainichi Nyorai.*
Copper; diam 39.4 cm. Hyōzu Shrine, Shiga Prefecture.

from their size, they were probably kept in small shrines used for family devotion. The reliquary is of elaborate workmanship, with gilt copper base and stand and five crystal balls representing the five deities of the Kasuga Shrine mounted on the backs of eight small deer.

Embroidered banners of the kind shown in Plate 38 were hung both inside and outside Buddhist halls as ornaments, and during the centuries of Buddhist-Shintō amalgamation, they came to be used in a similar fashion in Shintō sanctuaries. The origin of the wreathlike ornaments called *keman,* such as the one in Plate 39, is said to lie in the Indian practice of dedicating wreaths of flowers to the Buddha. The one preserved in the Hyōzu Shrine in Shiga Prefecture is made of gilt copper and is inscribed with the Siddham letter representing Dainichi Nyorai in the center. From the back it gives the appearance of a *mishotai.* The presence of such ornaments, pagodas, and other works of Buddhist inspiration in Shintō establishments gives some indication of the degree of the intermingling of the two faiths.

3

Shintō Sculpture

As the emphasis on nature, the predominant characteristic of early Shintō, gradually gave way to emphasis on shrine establishments in early Heian times, primitive popular cults underwent radical transformations in both spiritual and ritual terms. During this period the foundations of later shrine architecture, beliefs, and rituals were laid. The terms "natural Shintō" *(shizen shintō)* and "shrine Shintō" *(shaden shintō)* have been used frequently to distinguish between the religion of pre- and post-Nara times; they do not, however, take into account the most notable phenomenon in Shintō's development—its complete permeation by courtly elements as a result of its close relationship with the imperial court. Consequently, its ceremonies, architectural style, and even sculpture strongly reflect court customs and dress. The statues of Hachiman and the goddesses Nakatsu-hime and

Empress Jingū (Plates 40, 41, 42) in the Yakushi-ji at Nara exemplify this trend.

The Hachiman Triads

Hachiman, precursor of the rapprochement between Shintō and Buddhism, was invited to Yakushi-ji as its tutelary deity as early as the ninth century. He was enshrined in a subsidiary Shintō sanctuary on the grounds of this temple, one of the flourishing centers of Buddhist culture in the capital of Nara. The wooden Hachiman triad, designated a National Treasure and generally thought to have been made during the Jōgan era (859–77), is one of the oldest extant examples of Shintō sculpture. All the figures are carved from a single block of wood and painted, and are rather small in scale—they average only 36 centimeters in height.

40. *Nakatsu-hime, one of a Hachiman triad. Painted wood; ht 36.7 cm. Heian period. Yasumigaoka Hachiman Shrine, Yakushi-ji, Nara.*

41. *Hachiman in the guise of a monk (Sōgyō Hachiman), one of a triad. Painted wood; ht 39.7 cm. Heian period. Yasumigaoka Hachiman Shrine, Yakushi-ji, Nara.*

Both the goddesses (Plates 40 and 42), seated with one knee raised, have their hair hanging in folds over each shoulder and in back, and wear green T'ang-style robes with red highlights. Their solemn facial expression, manner of dress and its decoration, and handling of the folds of drapery reflect the sculptural tradition of the Jōgan era. Their light lacquer coating of flesh-colored skin, black painted hair, and pronounced eyebrows suggest the appearance of court ladies of the time.

Plates 43 and 47–49 depict three other ancient sculptures of Hachiman together with a single figure of Wakamiya Hachiman kept in the Kyoto Tō-ji. Hachiman was revered as the temple's tutelary deity at an early date because its founder, Kōbō Daishi (774–835), had deep faith in him. The figures were hidden from public view in the Miei-dō, where Kōbō Daishi's por-

trait sculpture is kept today. The Wakamiya Hachiman is rather small, but the three other figures, all over 100 centimeters in height, are imposing. The trinity was carved from a single block of wood that may have been a segment of a sacred tree. It is doubtful that they were made during the founder's lifetime, but since on stylistic grounds they seem to have been made shortly afterward, the temple tradition that they are copies of earlier images made according to his instructions is plausible. Their appearance—cross-legged posture and hand positions that are probably ritual gestures—as well as their carving and dress closely resemble the Buddhist sculpture of the time.

The figure of Wakamiya Hachiman is often mistakenly identified as Takeshi-uchi no Sukune, a minister who served under five emperors from about 355 to 394 and was renowned for his longevity. The statue

42. *Empress Jingū, one of a Hachiman triad. Painted wood; ht 35.5 cm. Heian period. Yasumigaoka Hachiman Shrine, Yakushi-ji, Nara.*

is naked but for a formal hat and scepter *(shaku)* and is extremely slender, since it was originally dressed in real robes. This is probably the oldest naked sculpture in Japan, although there are a number of others made in the Kamakura period, when this concept took firm hold, such as those of Benzai-ten, goddess of literature and music, in the Tsurugaoka Hachiman Shrine and in the Enoshima Benzai-ten Shrine. Even Shōtoku-taishi, the semideified imperial prince who played a vital role in the establishment of Buddhist culture, was commonly portrayed in the nude and dressed in elaborate robes on special occasions.

The Matsuno-o and Hayatama Figures

When the capital was moved to Kyoto in 794, several shrines in the area gained new prominence.

Among them was the Matsuno-o Shrine established in 701 by the Hata clan, mainland immigrants who had settled in the Kyoto area. Three figures of the Jōgan era—one female and two male—are kept here. Their exact identity is not known, but the older, more autocratic of the two male *kami* may be Oyamagui no Mikoto, the tutelary deity of Mount Hiei, which overlooks the shrine. The figures represent an elderly and a youthful man and a robust, matronly woman. The older *kami* (Plate 46) wears a hat with a short crown and a soft robe in the old style; the woman is dressed in a T'ang-style robe (Plates 10 and 52); and both have an awesome appearance. All are seated, made in the single-woodblock manner, and painted. Although much of the color has peeled off, traces of cinnabar red, which since antiquity was thought to have magical protective powers, are still visible.

43. *Goddess, one of a Hachiman triad. Painted wood; ht 113 cm. Heian period. Tō-ji, Kyoto.*

The special regard for this color is indicated both by archeological finds, such as weapons, ritual clay implements, and figures, and by literary sources. The *Nihon Shoki* has an account of Emperor Jimmu's expedition to eastern Japan in which he is said to have had clay containing cinnabar red cast into a river in Yamato and then predicted the outcome of a battle by the appearance of the fish killed in the poisoned water. It is also said that when Empress Jingū was about to leave on a punitive expedition to Korea, a red color from Niu in Yamato was used to paint her armor. Furthermore, a passage dated the eighth month of the year 938 in the *Honchō Seiki,* a historical document covering the years 935 through 1154, describes male and female figures called "*kami* of the crossroads" that were painted cinnabar red, and placed at every street corner in Kyoto.

Medieval Japanese also believed statues to be endowed with mystical powers, and unusual circumstances involving them were often the occasion of special rituals and offerings. The *Chūyūki,* the diary of Fujiwara no Munetada, a prominent member of the Fujiwara clan, states that in the spring of 1132 when the scepter fell from the hand of the male figure in the Matsuno-o Shrine in Kyoto, offerings were made and an oracle invoked. About the same time, whenever a crack developed in the sculpture of Fujiwara no Kamatari, the member of that family to whom the name was first granted, the court was informed, splendid offerings were made, and religious rites performed.

Paintings of the twelve gods of Kumano are described in Chapter 8, but there are also seven sculptures enshrined in the Hayatama Shrine, all of which have been designated National Treasures. These figures,

44. *Zemmyō Nyoshin. Painted wood; ht 31 cm. Zemmyō Nyoshin was adopted as a guardian deity of the Kōzan-ji because of her role in the Kegon Engi, the legends that describe the origin of the Kegon sect of Buddhism in Korea. The statue was carved in a Buddhist style by a member of the Kei school of sculptors. Kamakura period, twelfth century. Kōzan-ji, Kyoto.*

45. *Byakukō-shin. Painted wood; ht 42 cm. Originally an Indian goddess embodying the purity of the snows of the Himalayas, Byakukō-shin was adopted as a guardian deity in Buddhism. The monk Myō-e made her one of the Shintō guardians of the Kegon-sect monastery of Kōzan-ji and commissioned this work, which was sculpted in the strongly Sung-influenced Buddhist style of the Kamakura period. Kamakura period, twelfth century. Kōzan-ji, Kyoto.*

46. *Male deity (hikogami). Painted wood; ht 98 cm. Although figures in Shintō imagery are often characterized by youthfulness and* ▷
courtliness, reflecting the reverence for life inherent in the religion, others, such as this one, suggest the equally deep respect for the hermit or ascetic, whose other-worldliness, simplicity, and age-worn face seem to embody the spirit of a deity. Mid-ninth century. Matsuno-o Shrine, Kyoto.

47. Hachiman in the guise of a monk (Sōgyō Hachiman), one of a triad. Painted wood; ht 109 cm. Heian period. Tō-ji, Kyoto.

48. Goddess, one of a Hachiman triad. Painted wood; ht 112 cm. Heian period. Tō-ji, Kyoto.

all of which were made in the single-woodblock technique, are yet in comparatively good condition. They seem to have been uniformly painted with a thin coat of yellow, but this may actually be due to peeling and fading. Most impressive and oldest among them are the statues of Kumano Hayatama Okami and his female companion Kumano Fusumi Okami, illustrated in Plates 53 and 54. Both were probably made in the early Fujiwara period. Seated, like most early Shintō figures, they wear opulent robes under which their arms are folded. Hayatama Okami has a regal bearing and in fact wears a tall crown. His facial features are rather large and his ears elongated like those of a Buddha or Bodhisattva. Kumano Fusumi O-kami matches her companion in size and conveys an impression of abundance like the statue of the goddess in the Matsuno-o Shrine (Plates 10, 52).

The Yoshino Mikumari Sculptures

The Mikumari Shrine, the abode of a water deity, is located on a ridge of Mount Yoshino commonly called Hanayagura (the Flowered Turret) in a region renowned throughout Japan for its cherry trees. Even Emperor Godaigo (r. 1318–39), who removed his court here just before the Great Wars of Succession, was inspired to write a poem reflecting both his surprise at the sight of cherry blossoms near the Seson-ji temporary palace and his nostalgia for Kyoto.

> Even here in a cloudland
> Cherry trees have come to bloom . . .
> When all the while
> I thought this place was nothing more
> Than a lodging for the night.

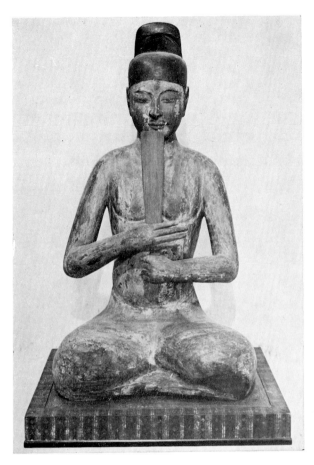

49. *Wakamiya Hachiman. Painted wood. Heian period. Tō-ji, Kyoto.*

The beauty of the setting seems to have changed little since those days, and even now the bell of Yoshino, one of the three famous bells of the Yamato region, continues to tell of its eight hundred years of history.

Throughout Japan, the origins of deities who control irrigation can be traced back to antiquity, and the history of their development is inseparable from that of the birth of farming in a particular region. Katsuragi no Mikumari, Uda no Mikumari, and Tsuge no Mikumari, in their role as gods of rain and water, all had considerable influence in ancient farming in the Yamato plains. The *kami* of the mountain peaks and plains, Mikumari no Kami and Yamaguchi no Kami, have always had a special place in the hearts of farmers, as have the deities Mizu Hanome, a water goddess, and others associated with the Niu River in Yamato.

The name Mikumari, ubiquitous among deities associated with water, was originally read *mizu-kubari*, which means water-parting or watershed. The goddess Mikomori Myōjin, although revered as a protector of children, seems to have emerged from a further corruption of the word *mikumari*.

In the Yoshino Mikumari Shrine are sculptures of more than twenty *kami*, among whom one of the best known is Ninigi no Mikoto, the grandson of Amaterasu Omikami. The most beautiful of all the sculptures is undoubtedly the figure of Tamayori-hime, reproduced in Plates 55 and 56. She is attended by two other goddesses, one to each side, and the triad is known collectively as the Komori San-nyoshin or the Three Protectresses of Children. According to the inscription inside the joined-woodblock figure of Tamayori-hime, it was made in 1251. The *Kojiki* introduces

龍田明神

50. *Tatsuta Myōjin. Detail of one of six painted cypress-wood panels. Painted in 1295 by the artist Gyōgon of the Buddhist painting atelier of Nara, this work is a fine example of yamato-e-style figure painting in Shintō art. The tutelary deity of the Tatsuta River in Nara Prefecture, Tatsuta Myōjin is shown here seated on a platform before a screen depicting the red-leafed maple trees for which the river is renowned. His dress and demeanor are that of a member of the court aristocracy, an illustration of the degree of court influence on artistic conventions even in religious art. Yasumigaoka Hachiman Shrine, Yakushi-ji, Nara.*

51. *Reizei Tamechika:* Butchō Sonshō Darani Shimmeibutsuda Kōrin Mandala. *Colors on silk; ht 150 cm. This long composition is dominated by a large treasure pagoda supported by a ring of lions, around which thirty-three Buddhist and Shintō deities are gathered. The glow of the Sonshō Darani (a magic prayer formula) inscribed on the pagoda is handled with great refinement. According to the inscription on the lower portion of the painting, it was executed by Tamechika, an artist active in the revival of the yamato-e style, in 1863. Okura Foundation, Tokyo.*

52. *Female deity. Painted wood; ht 87 cm. Heian period. Matsuno-o Shrine, Kyoto. (See also Plates 10, 46)*

her as the daughter of the sea deity Watatsumi no Kami and the mother of Emperor Jimmu, the first emperor of Japan. Her multilayered robe, painted in delicate colors, is handled very realistically, and her tranquil, somewhat sentimental face is reminiscent of a Nō mask.

The Tōdai-ji Hachiman and Other Kamakura Statues

Two sculptural styles were prevalent in Shintō sculpture from the Kamakura period on—the continuation of Heian trends, and the development of realistic portraitlike imagery. The statue of Sōgyō Hachiman (Plate 57) in Tōdai-ji follows the iconographic models for Hachiman imagery established during the Heian

period: In all its details, this life-size figure is in complete conformity with the painting of the god in the Jingō-ji (Plate 100). He is dressed in a monk's robe with a distant-mountain pattern, holds a staff in his right hand and a rosary in his left, and is seated on a lotus pedestal. The statue, however, is made in the joined-woodblock technique and is highly realistic, and in this sense differs fundamentally from most of the Heian-period Shintō statues discussed above.

Inside the cavity of the figure is a long inscription that begins with the words, "Enshrined in the Hachiman-gū of Tōdai-ji; eye-opening ceremony performed on the twenty-seventh day of the eleventh month of the year 1201. . . ." The eye-opening ceremony, a practice common in Buddhist circles, meant endowing the figure with spiritual life by painting in or inserting

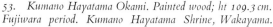

53. *Kumano Hayatama Okami. Painted wood; ht 109.3 cm. Fujiwara period. Kumano Hayatama Shrine, Wakayama.*

54. *Kumano Fusumi Okami. Painted wood; ht 106.5 cm. Fujiwara period. Kumano Hayatama Shrine, Wakayama.*

its eyes. The inscription refers to Tōdai-ji's Tamuke-yama Hachiman Shrine, destroyed in the Nara fire during the Jijō era (1177–81) and rebuilt in 1197. It was probably to furnish the rebuilt shrine that in 1201 the Buddhist sculptor Kaikei presented this figure, which he had made with the help of more than twenty assistants from the temple.

Plate 58 shows a standing statue of Izu-san Gongen with a Buddhist priest's stole over his shoulder and a nobleman's headdress. His somewhat informal attire is more typical of portrait sculptures than of Shintō imagery, and his plump face seems to reflect the Kamakura tendency toward marked realism. It is believed that he formerly held a short sword in his left hand and a scepter in his right. Also known as Sōtō-san Gongen since the mountain in Shizuoka Prefecture of

which he is the resident deity goes by both this name and Izu-san, he is one of the many *kami* whose origins have been obscured by Buddhist influence. In fact, a local fourteenth-century chronicle, the *Izu no Kuni Shinkaichō*, gives his name as Shōichi Sengen Daibosatsu and the Thousand-armed Kannon as his *honji-butsu*, clear indications of how deeply his history has been affected by Buddhism. In addition, the figure is kept in the Hannya-in, a Buddhist temple associated with the Izu Gongen Shrine, and is said to have been the guardian deity of the temple annalist.

During the Kamakura period both Izu-san Gongen and Hakone Gongen, the deity of another mountain region in Shizuoka Prefecture, acquired national status when the Minamoto feudal government made offerings twice yearly and even the shogun himself made

55. *Tamayori-hime. Painted wood; ht 83 cm. 1251. Yoshino Mikumari Shrine, Nara Prefecture.*

regular pilgrimages there. The prosperity of their shrines was consequently sustained by the government.

The style of this figure of Izu-san Gongen may have served as a model for the images of Ebisu, the god of wealth, that gained widespread popularity in later times. Other Kamakura-period wooden figures, such as the one of Tenjin, the deified spirit of the minister Sugawara Michizane, in the Egara Tenjin Shrine in Kamakura, also seem to be related to this one.

Zemmyō Nyoshin and Byakukō-shin

Japanese monks who went to China in search of Buddhist scriptures and art brought back many deities of both Buddhist and Taoist origins whom they had adopted as special guardians during their journeys. These gods generally came to be revered as attendants to Japanese divinities and sometimes became the objects of new cults. They were installed in subsidiary shrines within the temple compounds as tutelary gods and were worshiped along with the resident *kami*. It also became customary to make paintings or sculptures of them to place in the temple on the occasion of important rites, such as those of Shiragi (Shinra) Myōjin (Plate 76), and of Matara-jin and Sekizan Myōjin (Plates 70 and 71). Among the most popular of these foreign deities are two goddesses—Zemmyō Nyoshin and Byakukō-shin (Plates 44 and 45)—enshrined in 1225 with the gods of Kasuga and Sumiyoshi Shrines by the monk Myō-e (1173–1232) in a subsidiary shrine of the Kōzan-ji in Kyoto.

56. *Tamayori-hime. Detail of figure.*

Zemmyō Nyoshin's connection with this temple derives from her role as heroine of the *Kegon Engi,* a collection of tales about the origins of the Kegon sect. The tales are well known from their depiction in illustrated narrative scrolls kept in the Kōzan-ji, which is a Kegon temple. One of the principal legends concerns a Korean monk named Ui-sang (Gishō in Japanese), the seventh-century founder of this sect in Korea, who met a beautiful lady named Shan-miao (Zemmyō in Japanese) while studying Kegon Buddhism in China. Zemmyō fell in love with this devoted monk, and later, when he had to return to Korea, was so broken-hearted that she determined to follow him. Due to her pure love and deep faith in Buddhism, she was transformed into a dragon, in which guise she was able to guide his ship to Korea.

The image of Zemmyō in Plate 44 was made in 1224 by the sculptor Tankei (1173–1256), a member of the Buddhist Kei school. His Buddhist affiliations are quite apparent in both the technique and style of the figure. Inspired by the description of her just before she cast herself into the sea to follow in the wake of the ship bearing Gishō to Korea, the artist portrayed the goddess standing on a rocky crag, holding a box of jewels for the monk. Her dress is distinctly Chinese, but her headdress is like that worn by Buddhist deities. Both the highly detailed carving and the somewhat sentimental realism of her face are typical of the Kamakura period.

Tankei's background in Buddhist imagery is even more marked in his sculpture of Byakukō-shin (Plate 45). Though originally an Indian earth goddess said

57. *Kaikei: Hachiman in the guise of a monk (Sōgyō Hachiman). Painted wood; ht 87.1 cm. 1201. Tōdai-ji, Nara.*

to embody the purity of the snows of the Himalayas, she was assimilated into the Buddhist pantheon, and later, perhaps due to her initial role as a nature deity, adopted as a Shintō guardian of the Kōzan-ji. Her portrayal here seems to stem from images of Taishaku-ten or Indra in ancient Indian mythology, shown as an attendant figure in Buddhist art. In particular, her robe and slightly fleshy, moustached face bear a close resemblance to representations of this Indian Buddhist deity. Her body, however, is completely white in keeping with her original role.

Honji-Butsu and Other Sculptures

The intermingling of Shintō and Buddhism that first manifested itself in the Nara period in the build-

ing of Buddhist temples on Shintō shrine compounds later led to the creation of Shintō sculpture. In time, the relationship between the two religions and their deities was systematized in what is generally termed the *honji-suijaku* theory, according to which Shintō gods are manifestations or subordinate forms *(gongen* or *suijaku)* of Buddhist deities *(honji)*. This is the origin of the term *honji-suijaku* art.

The allotment of Buddhist counterparts to all *kami* began in the Heian period; by Kamakura times, the relationship was fairly well established throughout the country, although some documents express different opinions about the correspondences. Thus either Amida or Shaka was considered the *honji* of the deity of the central sanctuary of Iwashimizu Hachiman Shrine, and at Kasuga, both Shaka and Fukū-kenjaku ap-

58. Izu-san Gongen. Wood; ht 50.1 cm. Kamakura period. Hannya-in, Shizuoka Prefecture.

59. Yakushi Nyorai (honji). Wood; ht 30 cm. Fujiwara period. Isobe Shrine, Shiga Prefecture.

peared as that of the *kami* in the Ichi no Miya. *Honji-butsu* were often enshrined in halls built for that purpose within the shrine precincts. Moreover, the staff associated with such Buddhist establishments, which had a completely different religious role from that of the Shintō sanctuaries, bore special titles distinguishing them from the Shintō priests. When the two creeds were separated in 1868, many images of the Buddhist *honji* at shrines were destroyed. Others, however, were transferred to neighboring temples where they still survive, although in many cases those without inscriptions remain unidentified.

Among the statues of Buddhist *honji* that can be linked with their Shintō counterparts, one of the most prominent is the wooden image of the Nyoirin Kannon at the Daigo-ji (Plate 60); an inscribed bronze

mirror from the same temple also depicts Nyoirin (Plate 35). This Esoteric form of Kannon, holding the jewel and wheel that symbolize supernatural ability to achieve all goals, is the *honji* of the goddess Seiryū Gongen. The cult of Seiryū, which is discussed further in Chapter 4, was originally brought from China by Kōbō Daishi of the Shingon sect. The concept of the goddess was then fused with that of the ancient tutelary deity of Mount Daigo, and with the development of the *honji-suijaku* theories, the Nyoirin Kannon was adopted as her *honji*. The basis of the Daigo cult would therefore seem to lie in the fusion of beliefs concerning three separate deities: the early and primitive local mountain god, the Seiryū Gongen from the mainland, and the Esoteric Buddhist form of Kannon.

The *honji-butsu* of Isobe Shrine (Shiga Prefecture)

60. *Nyoirin Kannon,* honji *of Seiryū Gongen. Fujiwara period. Daigo-ji, Kyoto.*

reproduced in Plate 59 is barely thirty centimeters high and is not lacquered like most Buddhist sculptures; rather, it is of plain wood covered with patterns in gold leaf. This Fujiwara-period image seems to imitate Shintō sculpture in its use of plain wood, but it has the beauty of a piece of craftsmanship rather than that of a piece of sculpture. Its body, the pedestal with overhanging drapery, and the double halo with a carved flower pattern convey an impression of sumptuousness heightened by the fleshy, rotund face and powerful torso. Since the image from the base of the pedestal to the top of the mandorla (halo) is only sixty centimeters high, it must have been installed in a small shrine.

Plate 61 shows the *honji* of the Oda Shrine in Omi Hachiman, Shiga Prefecture: a seated sculpture

of Dainichi Nyorai with his hands folded in meditative posture. It is a Fujiwara-period single-woodblock sculpture about one meter in height; the figure wears a crown in the center of which five Buddhas are carved in relief, and has shoulder-length hair. The shrines in Shiga Prefecture are almost all deeply permeated by ideas of the Tendai sect, since Mount Hiei is not far away, and this figure seems to reflect the influence of the Esoteric branch of the school.

Koma-inu

Scholars have long studied the origins of a pair of carved animals generally likened to lions or Pekinese dogs and called *koma-inu,* which are found at the entrance of a shrine or shrine compound. Numerous ex-

61. *Dainichi Nyorai* (honji). *Painted wood; ht 100 cm. Fujiwara period. Oda Shrine, Shiga Prefecture.*

planations for this custom have been offered, among them a legend that dogs were used to lead the army during Empress Jingū's expedition to Korea in the third century. The most plausible historical explanation, however, is that the custom derives from the use of sculpted lions and lion-dogs as accessory supports for screens in mainland palaces. This Chinese practice seems to have been adopted in Japan in T'ang times (618–907), when carved stone lions were also commonly placed at imperial mausoleums, which may account for the Japanese designation of "T'ang," or simply "Chinese," lion for any such statue. In addition, since many elements of Chinese culture were also transmitted to Japan via Korea, these creatures are also called *koma-inu*, which means Korean dog when written with different characters.

Characteristic of these pairs of figures is the fact that one dog's mouth is closed and the other's open. This has been interpreted to mean the beginning and the end—the alpha and the omega. The origins of this feature are said to lie in the Heian period when the lion sculptures used as screen supports were made so that the one on the right had its mouth open and the one on the left had it closed.

Records concerning palace practices such as the *Kimpi-shō* (1221) and the *Zatsuyō-shō* describe *koma-inu* used at the court. The earliest document referring to their use at shrines may be the *Kōdai Ki,* compiled in 1084, which records that in 1039, gold and silver lions were offered to Ise Shrine. In fact, their introduction into shrines probably dates from Fujiwara times, when the court exerted a strong influence on Shintō

62. *Pair of* koma-inu. *Wood. Early Kamakura period. Taihō Shrine, Shiga Prefecture.*

culture. With the development of shrine Shintō (*sha-den shintō*), they came to be placed in the outside cor-ridor of the sanctuary for both protection and decora-tion in the same way that stone figures of men and horses had been earlier.

The variety of *koma-inu* seen today before shrines is the result of divergent influences from China. On a stylistic basis they can be divided into two broad categories according to whether they are related to the ancient style derived from T'ang China or to that which developed in Sung (960–1279) and post-Sung times. Among the latter, many are made of stone; the pair carved by the Sung sculptor Yin, today in the Great South Gate of the Tōdai-ji, are examples of this type. Those in the Chikuzen Munagata Shrine and

Kurama-yuki Shrine have been designated Important Cultural Properties. Included within the former cate-gory are pairs that still resemble screen supports. Gen-erally the right one is painted gold and has its mouth open, and the left one is painted silver and has its mouth closed. Reproduced in Plate 62 is a pair of renowned *koma-inu* from the early Kamakura period belonging to the Taihō Shrine in the city of Kusatsu, Shiga Prefecture. Gold and silver have been applied as the first coat of color and the fur has been tinted green. Although crystal eyes are frequent in works of this period, these are carved. The one with the closed mouth has an air of fierceness and pent-up energy, but both are like fighters sizing up their opponents before a fight.

4

Paintings of Shintō Deities

The amalgam of Buddhism and Shintō is, of course, reflected in painting as well as in sculpture, along with the influence of court practices and styles. In addition, the subjects of Shintō paintings were not only the *kami* and their *honji,* but the forms in which deities manifested themselves to men. Accounts of visions interwoven into narratives and legends were illustrated in paintings made for devotional use.

Panel Paintings

The handsome color image of a male deity in Plate 50 is a section from one of the six painted panels that formed part of the transom in the Hachiman Shrine at the entrance to the compound of the Yakushi-ji in Nara. Executed on cypress wood, they depict twenty-two gods and goddesses from various shrines. According to an inscription on the back, they were painted in the spring of 1295 by the Nara artist Gyōgon to replace the damaged original late eleventh-century paintings on sliding doors *(shōji-e)*. The figures in the southern hall of the shrine all face to the right and those in the northern hall to the left, so that their gazes meet.

The god shown in Plate 50 is identified as Tatsuta Myōjin, probably originally worshiped as a wind god. His facial expression is rather amiable in comparison with most *kami*. Since he is dressed in a soft robe with a *tatewaku* pattern rather than in the stiff type that later became popular, this work would seem to be based on the earlier eleventh-century version. (Examples of the formal attire of subsequent periods can be seen in Plates 78, 79, and 122.) The red-leafed tree on

63. Gyōgon: Panel paintings of Shintō gods. Wood. 1295. Yasumigaoka Hachiman Shrine, Yakushi-ji, Nara.

the screen behind him is typical of the Tatsuta River of which he is the deity.

Illustrated in Plates 63 and 64 are sections from two other panels. The *kami* in monk's robes is identified in the small label to the right of his head as Yanagimoto Myōjin. *Yanagi* means willow in Japanese, and he is appropriately portrayed before a willow tree. The names of the other male deity with a more autocratic look and of the two goddesses in Plate 64 are not legible.

Examples of panel paintings of Shintō deities are not exclusive to the Nara area. Another group is depicted in the Hōshaku-ji in Kyoto, a temple said to have been founded in 727 at the order of Emperor Shōmu. Originally the fifteen tutelary *gongen* of the temple were portrayed, but these panels were destroyed by fire. The present works, executed on cy-

press boards on the back of which are inscribed the date 1286, are unfortunately in poor condition. Much of the coloring has peeled off, leaving only the black outlines of the figures. These include the familiar deities of the Kumano, Kitano, and Matsuno-o shrines, as well as Hachiman. The paintings in the Hōshaku-ji, those in the Yakushi-ji, as well as a later series from 1628 in the Hakone Shrine near Tokyo are particularly valuable because of their exact dating. It is also possible that the earlier panel paintings of *kami* may have influenced the development of portrayals of the thirty-six great poets of Japan *(kasen-e),* which are commonly executed on wooden plaques.

The Thirty Banshin

Another type of group image developed in the cult

64. Gyōgon: Panel paintings of Shintō goddesses. Wood. 1295. Yasumigaoka Hachiman Shrine, Yakushi-ji, Nara.

of the thirty *banshin* or tutelary deities of each day of the month. The concept of the thirty *banshin* evolved early in the Heian period due to the activities of Ennin (Jikaku Daishi, 794–864), the most renowned abbot of the Tendai sect after its founder. According to the Lotus Sutra, the principal scripture of this sect, vast spiritual merit could be accumulated by maintaining, reading, reciting, or copying this sacred text. Spurred by this directive, Ennin secluded himself in a cave on Mount Hiei and began to perform a rite called *Ichiji-sanrai,* in which every time he copied a single character of the scripture, he paid homage to the three treasures of Buddhism—the Buddha, his teachings, and the religious orders.

He began by copying the Lotus Sutra in eight scrolls with two scrolls of introduction and conclusion, seventy thousand characters in all. After three long years,

the finished work, given the name *Kompon Nyohō-kyō,* was enshrined in a small hall with the same name, the Kompon Nyohō-dō. As was customary, Ennin invited deities to protect the hall and its contents, and chose the thirty principal Shintō deities of Japan. Since each was responsible for its protection on one day of the thirty-day month, they were called the thirty *banshin,* or guardians. Even today there is a small sanctuary on one side of the mountain, near the Nyohō-dō, for the deity on daily guard duty.

In the medieval period, the concept of the *banshin* was adopted without any change by the Nichiren sect of Buddhism, named after its founder, who lived from 1222 to 1282. Nichiren also based his doctrines on the Lotus Sutra, and the belief in these guardian deities continued to live on in popular religion along with widespread devotion to this scripture.

65. Thirty Guardian Deities. *Colors on silk; ht 95 cm, w 40 cm. Danzan Shrine, Nara Prefecture.*

Paintings of the thirty deities in rows were executed on Mount Hiei and in temples of Nichiren affiliation, where they are still hung to protect the temple on the occasion of religious ceremonies. However, very few made as early as Kamakura times exist today; the majority date from the Muromachi to the Edo period. For the most part, earlier examples represent standing deities, whereas more recent ones depict them seated on platforms backed by three-paneled screens. Of the former, there is a charming example in the Danzan Shrine in Nara Prefecture (Plate 65) and a somewhat more formal one in the Homma Art Museum in Yamagata Prefecture (Plate 66). The one in the Hompō-ji in Kyoto (Plate 67) is typical of the more recent type. One of the most precious documents of its kind is a panel painting of the thirty *banshin* dated 1433

preserved in the Shirahige Shrine in the town of Moriyama in Shiga Prefecture.

A Late Shintō-Buddhist Mandala

An unusual painting executed just before the change of official policy toward Shintō and Buddhism in the late 1860s provides interesting insights into the personal devotion and inspiration of a devout Buddhist at this crucial time. This rather large composition (150 cm in length), reproduced in Plate 51, is today in the Okura Foundation collection in Tokyo. It depicts a group of thirty-three deities assembled around an elaborate pagoda supported by a ring of lions. To the left are seventeen Shintō gods and to the right, sixteen Buddhas and Bodhisattvas.

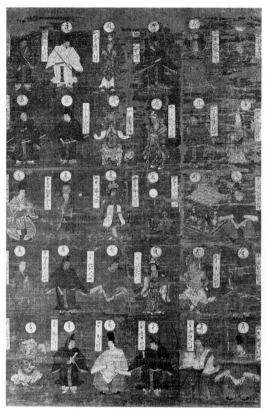

66. Thirty Guardian Deities. *Homma Art Museum, Yamagata Prefecture.*

67. Thirty Guardian Deities. *Colors on silk; ht 93 cm, w 37.9 cm. Hompō-ji, Kyoto.*

From the inscription beneath the pagoda we know that this work was made at the wish of a monk named Gankai and conceived independently of any particular scripture by his friend Reizei Tamechika, an artist active in reviving traditional modes of Japanese painting *(yamato-e)* and opposed to the military government then in power. Under suspicion by the government because of his loyalist leanings, in 1862 Tamechika sought refuge in a temple in Kii but was captured and assassinated two years later. Gankai had long had deep faith in the *Sonshō Darani,* a magic formula or prayer (dhāranī in Sanskrit) that extols the immense merits contained within the Buddha's cranial protuberance or *usnisa* and recommends copying, reciting, and preserving this text in order to accumulate spiritual merits. In 1854, he asked Tamechika to paint a *mandala* sym-

bolizing this formula. In addition, he had him write and print a related text in order to increase the spiritual merit he might obtain from the *dhāranī.* Under his friend's influence, Tamechika gradually developed a similar reverence toward this formula.

The origin of the seventeen *kami* and sixteen Buddhist deities is not very clear. The artist's source of inspiration may have been the Heaven of the Thirty-three Gods, a paradise described from early times in Indian Buddhist literature, and he may have substituted other gods to reflect the concepts of the Shintō-Buddhist synthesis. The identity of each is not certain either, but from the top, there are the three deities of the Ise, Hachiman, and Kasuga shrines, perhaps the most important in Japan, followed by Sannō Gongen —the male deity dressed in T'ang-style robes. The

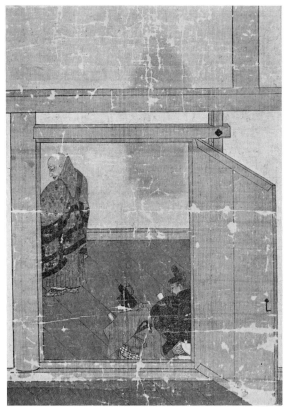

68. Manifestation of Hachiman at Usa. *Kamakura period. Ninna-ji, Kyoto.*

69. Vision of Seiryū Gongen. *Colors on silk; ht 84.8 cm, w 42.7 cm. Hatakeyama Museum, Tokyo.*

figure to his right cannot be identified. Below them are Kumano Gongen and Sumiyoshi Okami, both in the guise of old men; the goddess riding on a white fox, an animal which like the deer often served as an intermediary between gods and men, is probably Uga-shin, a deity of Buddhist origin assimilated into the Shintō pantheon. Next come Okuni-nushi no Mikoto, who in Shintō mythology is the master of the land, he who put the earth in order, and Ame no Uzume no Mikoto, whose lively dance enticed Amaterasu Omikami out of the cave. The archer standing next to a white fox is Kurainadama no Mikoto, and the animal-faced deity below him is Sarudahiko no Mikoto. The identity of the helmeted soldier in armor on a horse is unknown. The figure dressed in formal black attire appears to be Kitano Tenjin, but the next

one cannot be identified. Finally, in the lower corner, Bishamon-ten, the guardian of the north, and En no Gyōja, founder of the ascetic Shugendō sect, and his child attendant are visible.

The Shintō and Buddhist gods portrayed here are all modeled after works of art today dispersed throughout Japan, with which only an artist with Tamechika's knowledge of ancient *yamato-e*-style paintings could have been familiar. The deities to the left and right sides are not related to one another as *honji* and *suijaku*, but are simply depicted as a group descending to admire and protect the *Sonshō Darani,* which is written within a large circle on the main body of a particularly beautiful pagoda. Since the painting's coloring and condition are excellent, this modern work is a valuable and rare document.

70. Matara-jin. *Nakamura Collection.*　　　71. Sekizan Myōjin. *Edo period. Sekizan Zen-in, Kyoto.*

Hachiman, Seiryū Gongen, and Others

The belief that a deity could manifest himself on earth in his own form or in other guises was particularly strong in late Heian popular religion. In one legend, the deity of Kashima now enshrined in the Kasuga Ichi no Miya appeared on earth and rode on the back of a white deer to the foot of Mount Mikasa (Plate 81). In another well-known legend, Kōbō Daishi (774–835, founder of the Shingon sect of Buddhism) encountered the goddess of Mount Kōya, Niu Myōjin (or Niutsu-hime Myōjin), shown in Plate 74, and received her permission to build a monastic center there. The *Ryōjin Hishō,* which is a late Heian anthology, contains numerous unpretentious songs expressing the spirit of belief in such manifestations. One of the bal-

lads contained in it describes this with great charm:

> Buddha is always present
>> Wherever we are,
> Yet he is not real to our sight,
>> A sad regret.
> When there are no sounds of men,
>> In the light of dawn,
> Then faintly, in our dreams,
>> He will appear.

This deep-felt belief in the actual existence of Buddhist and Shintō gods was a continual source of hope for men of the medieval period. Naturally, if a person's profound faith resulted in his gaining the object of a prayer or a vision of a deity, the populace became all the more convinced of the deity's actual existence.

72. Mikomori Sansho Nyoshin. *Fujioka Collection.*

73. Mikomori Sansho Nyoshin. *Yamato Bunkakan, Nara.*

From the Kamakura period on, accounts of visions were assimilated into religious narratives and illustrated in the plastic arts. The portrayals of Kasuga Wakamiya (Plate 82), that of Hachiman (Plate 98), and of Seiryū Gongen (Plate 69) all depict forms in which these *kami* manifested themselves to human beings. The story of the Kasuga Myōjin shown in Plate 97 is discussed in Chapter 5; the events surrounding the appearances of Hachiman and Seiryū Gongen, however, require further amplification.

The image of two courtiers kneeling in the corner of a shrine before the figure of a monk (Plate 68) is based on an account of great historical interest. One of the courtiers is Wake no Kiyomaro (733–99), who was sent by Empress Shōtoku to the Usa Hachiman Shrine to consult the *kami* on an affair of tradition-

breaking consequence. At that time, the Empress had complete confidence in a monk named Dōkyō, to whom she was considering ceding the throne; but afraid to break the chain of imperial authority descending from the gods themselves, she sought the advice of Hachiman. While praying at the shrine, in the middle of the night Wake no Kiyomaro had a vision of Hachiman in the guise of a monk walking across the room and received an oracle to the effect that the imperial line should not be broken. The discrepancy in size between Hachiman and his devotees reflects his divine status.

The portrayal of Seiryū Gongen (Plate 69) is associated with Kōbō Daishi, who brought this goddess from Mount Ch'ing-lung in China as a guardian of the Shingon sect. She was first worshiped in the Jingō-

74. **Niu Myōjin.** *Detail. Colors on silk; ht 79 cm, w 39.5 cm. Both this goddess and her son, generally depicted in the guise of a hunter, were adopted as special guardians of the monastic center founded by Kōbō Daishi on Mount Kōya, of which they are the tutelary deities. The word niu is of particular interest, since it recurs throughout Japan as a place name associated with the mining of mercury and the clans involved in this industry. Niu Myōjin may have originally been a kami worshiped by such families. As depicted here in the guise of a buxom court lady, she has a mysterious, distant air. Kamakura period. Kongōbu-ji, Wakayama Prefecture.*

75. Mikomori Sansho Nyo-
shin. *Kurisu Collection.*

(overleaf)

76.   Shiragi (Shinra) Myōjin. *Colors on silk; ht 86.4 cm, w 39.1 cm. Introduced by Chishō Daishi as a guardian of the Onjō-ji in* ▷
*Heian times, this bearded age-worn figure retains a markedly Chinese air. His hat, robe, chair, and open mouth—perhaps uttering a magic
formula—are especially revealing of his non-Japanese origins. Another deity and two child gods (dōji) are depicted at his feet. This as
well as several other portrayals of Shiragi Myōjin in this temple seem to have been inspired by images of the God of Fire, one of the
twelve gods of the elements in Buddhism. Early Muromachi period. Onjō-ji, Shiga Prefecture.*

77.   Kasuga Shrine Mandala. *Detail. Colors on silk; ht 65.4 cm, w 28.5 cm. Dark Mount Mikasa frames the simple structures of the* ▷
four Kasuga shrines surrounded by a sacred red fence broken by a small torii, *the characteristic shrine gateway. Simpler than most Kasuga
mandalas, it was probably executed before the great fire that destroyed much of Nara in 1180. Within the four golden circles above the
shrines are Siddham letters (a script used to write Sanskrit) representing the names of the* honji *of the four Kasuga deities. Kamakura period.
Nezu Art Museum, Tokyo.*

ji in Kyoto and then in the form of a rock atop Mount Daigo, where she had been combined with the primitive *kami* of the mountain. She is one of a number of deities imported from the mainland and adopted into the Shintō pantheon as protectors of Buddhist temples. In China, Seiryū Gongen was believed to have the form of a goddess, so in Shintō representations she is generally depicted as a lovely woman dressed in T'ang-style garments and carrying a magic jewel. In this painting she appears magnified in scale; she wears a gold jeweled crown and stands in front of a sliding door decorated with a landscape. The young girl in the foreground holds a book she has received from the goddess. The inscription above the scene indicates that the picture reproduces a dream the young woman had on the ninth day of the fourth month of 1204.

Matara-jin and Sekizan Myōjin on Mount Hiei (Plates 70 and 71) and Shiragi Myōjin (also called Shinra Myōjin), the tutelary deity of the Mii-dera on the shore of Lake Biwa (Plate 76), are gods of similar background whose worship developed in Esoteric circles in Japan. All three seem to derive from Taoist deities assimilated into the Buddhist pantheon in China and later introduced to Japan. Matara-jin was brought to Mount Hiei by Ennin, the Tendai monk famed for his travels in China, and seems to have been closely associated with Buddhist rituals involving music. Thus the painting reproduced here depicts him beating a drum while two attendants perform a dance before him. The constellation above his head, however, suggests that he may have originally been worshiped as a stellar deity. According to tradition, Sekizan Myōjin

78. *Toyotomi Hideyoshi as Toyokuni Daimyōjin. Saikyō-ji, Shiga Prefecture.*

79. *Tokugawa Ieyasu as Tōshō Daigongen. Sairin-ji, Ibaraki Prefecture.*

was initially revered on Mount Ch'ih in Shantung Province in China and later enshrined by Ennin in Mount Hiei's Sekizan Zen-in, where this painting is kept. Shiragi Myōjin's Chinese origin is quite apparent in his portrayal here. Such paintings of him were used as devotional images in Esoteric ceremonies.

The deification of emperors and influential leaders or members of the government is a phenomenon peculiar to the Shintō creed. The case of Sugawara Michizane, today worshiped in the Kitano Shrine in Kyoto and discussed in Chapter 1, is only one example. Plates 78 and 79 represent two more recent historical figures deified shortly after their death: the

unifier of feudal Japan, Toyotomi Hideyoshi (1536–98), and the first of the Tokugawa shoguns, Tokugawa Ieyasu (1542–1616). The former is venerated under the name Toyokuni Daimyōjin at the Hōkoku Shrine in Kyoto, where his tomb is located. In this work he is portrayed in formal dress, seated on a platform before a landscape screen. His penetrating gaze seems to convey his political and military acumen. Tokugawa Ieyasu, apotheosized as Tōshō Daigongen and worshiped at the Tōshōgū Shrine at Nikkō, is depicted seated at the entrance of a shrine in a manner reminiscent of representations of the thirty *banshin*.

5

Art of the Kasuga Cult

Most Japanese families whose origins can be traced back to ancient times have one or more tutelary deities believed to be their ancestors. The imperial family claims descent from the sun goddess Amaterasu Omikami; the Imbe clan is said to descend from the god Ame no Tomi no Mikoto, who persuaded the sun goddess to emerge from a cave to which she had retired, scandalized by the misconduct of her brother Susano-o no Mikoto. Similarly, the Fujiwara family claims as its ancestors Ame no Koyane no Mikoto, who also helped entreat Amaterasu Omikami to emerge from the cave, and his consort Himegami. The Fujiwara family shrine is the Kasuga Taisha in Nara, one of the best known of all Shintō sanctuaries, where the tutelary deities *(ujigami)* of the family are worshiped together with gods of the local area.

The Origins of Kasuga

The Fujiwara clan was originally known as Nakatomi until 669 when the emperor granted the influential minister Nakatomi no Kamako (614–69) the family name Fujiwara. The clan originated in the Hiraoka region of the old Kawachi Province to the east of modern Osaka. During the Kofun (Tumulus) period (third to the sixth centuries), they, like other groups bound by regional or family ties, worshiped their ancestors and local agricultural gods in rituals centered on the massive funeral mounds characteristic of this era. Prayers were generally addressed to a pair of male and female deities with whose help, it was believed, harvests would be abundant.

The fusion of this early agricultural cult with that

◁ *80.* Kasuga Shrine Mandala. *Detail. Colors on silk; ht 108 cm, w 49 cm. The cinnabar-colored shrine precincts, built at the foot of Mount Mikasa and surrounded by tall cedars, are executed with great precision in the traditional* yamato-e *style in this outstanding Kasuga mandala. The four simple structures depicted in Plate 77 can be seen to the left within the main compound; here they are part of an elaborate complex reflecting the evolution of Shintō from a simple nature worship to a state religion under the patronage and protection of powerful court families. On the upper portion of thi mandala, shown in Plate 89, are three sections of calligraphy by the Retired Emperor Kameyama (r. 1259–74); below these are the* honji-butsu *of five gods, each seated within a circle. Fourteenth century.*

of the clan ancestors or guardians led to such couples being regarded as *ujigami.* By the seventh century, the god Ame no Koyane no Mikoto and the goddess Himegami were established as the tutelary deities of the Nakatomi clan, and with the development of shrine Shintō, the Hiraoka Shrine was devoted to them.

The Fujiwaras moved with the court to the new capital at Nara in 709 and came to wield great power in the government. In order to retain the divine protection of their tutelary deities, they called them to the new city and selected Mount Mikasa, east of the palace, as the site of the family cult. This low, verdant slope had previously been worshiped as a sacred mountain by the clans living in the northern Yamato plains, and the Fujiwaras assimilated the clan gods of their predecessors.

The cult was further expanded by the inclusion of the *kami* Futsunushi no Mikoto of Katori in present-day Chiba Prefecture and Takemikazuchi no Mikoto of Kashima in nearby Ibaraki Prefecture. It is likely that they were introduced into the capital as war gods or guardians against further uprisings in the north, since in the eighth century northern Honshū had just been subjugated and these two deities were credited with the original pacification of the area. The establishment of the shrines to these four *kami* is said to have taken place in the Jingo-keiun era (767–70), and the private devotion of the Fujiwaras was thus transformed into a cult affecting the city and even the nation. The prosperity and decline of the Kasuga Shrines in later times reflected the expansion and contraction of the city of Nara as well as the fortunes of the Fujiwara clan.

82. Manifestation of Kasuga Wakamiya Incarnate as a Young Prince. *Frontispiece of the Kongō-hannya-kyō. Ht 26 cm, w 22 cm. This painting was discovered inside a sculpture of Monju Bosatsu seated on a lion carved by Kōen (b. 1207) and is said to represent a dream of the Nara monk Kyōgen just after the completion of the statue in which he saw the Kasuga dōji in the fields at Kasuga amid luxuriantly blooming cherry trees. 1273. Gotō Art Museum, Tokyo.*

◁ 81. Kasuga Deer Mandala. *Detail. Colors on silk; ht 137.6 cm, w 57 cm. This sacred Kasuga deer bears a saddle supporting a sakaki branch symbolizing the presence of Kasuga Myōjin (Takemikazuchi no Mikoto), who traveled on the back of this animal from Kashima to Mount Mikasa near Nara, which he chose as his new abode. The deer is realistically drawn, and the streamers hanging from the branches of the sacred sakaki seem to blow in the wind above the gleaming saddle decorated with gold foil. Kamakura period. Yōmei Library, Kyoto.*

83. *(left) Portrayal of the deity of Kashima. Colors on silk. Kasuga Shrine, Nara.*

84. *(right) Kasuga Deer Mandala. Colors on silk; ht 70 cm, w 27.9 cm. Miyaji Collection.*

As can be seen in Plates 77, 89, and 90, so-called Kasuga *mandalas* depict the sanctuaries devoted to these deities, who came to be known collectively as the Four Kasuga Gongen, although occasionally a fifth shrine—the *wakamiya*—is also included. The *wakamiya* is a type of subsidiary shrine often devoted to a child of the *kami* in the principal sanctuary. In a broader sense, it symbolizes the concept of youthfulness and rebirth reflected in the Shintō ceremony called *mi-are*, in which a deity's powers are rejuvenated. The term *wakamiya* is also used to designate the god enshrined in such a sanctuary. At Kasuga, however, the relationship between the main shrine and the *wakamiya* is not genealogical; rather, it is a vestige of ancient local forms of worship. In early times Mount Mikasa probably had sanctuaries at its peak and foot called "mountain shrine" and "village shrine," respectively,

(overleaf)

85. Iwashimizu Shrine Mandala. *Within this depiction of the* ▷ *whole of the Otokoyama Iwashimizu Shrine near Kyoto, including the Buddhist establishments scattered here and there, considerable attention is paid to landscape elements. Except for the fact that it includes the structures at the foot of the mountain, it closely resembles the scene in the* Ippen Shōnin Eden *reproduced in Plate 104. Kamakura period. Okura Foundation, Tokyo.*

86. Iwashimizu Hachiman Mandala. *This Iwashimizu Hachiman* mandala, *done in the same overall-view style as that shown in Plate 85, depicts on an even broader scale the whole of the shrine against a sweeping background of landscape. The way in which the buildings are placed in a natural, scenic setting gives this* mandala *value not only as a painting of refined and delicate quality but also as an architectural record of the shrine complex at the height of its prosperity. The shrine tradition is that it was produced in the early years of the Jōwa era (1345–50) and that it was long used as an object of worship. Early Muromachi period. Nezu Art Museum, Tokyo.*

but gradually the mountain came to be considered a god-body *(shintai-zan)* needing no sanctuary. Consequently, today the mountain itself represents the mountain shrine and the *wakamiya* corresponds to the village shrine.

Any discussion of the Kasuga cult would not be complete without considering the shrine's relationship to the adjacent Kōfuku-ji, the Fujiwaras' tutelary Buddhist temple. The Kōfuku-ji emerged from one of the clan temples called Yamashina-dera built at the order of Fujiwara no Kamatari (Nakatomi no Kamako) in Yamashiro Province in the hills east of Kyoto. This temple was later transferred to the southern Yamato plains and became the Umayasaka-dera; finally, when it was moved to the new capital at Nara, it was renamed Kōfuku-ji.

Both the proximity of the two religious establish-

87. *The deities of Kasuga riding deer. Detail of a painted box. Later Kamakura period. Tamabayashi Collection.*

ments and the general tendency toward Buddhist-Shintō admixture in Kamakura times led to the attribution of Buddhist *honji* or "true forms" to each of the *kami* of the Kasuga Shrine. Takemikazuchi no Mikoto of the Ichi no Miya was given Fukū-kenjaku or Shaka Nyorai; Futsunushi no Mikoto of the Ni no Miya, Yakushi Nyorai; Ame no Koyane no Mikoto of the San no Miya, Jizō; and Himegami of the Shi no Miya, Jūichimen Kannon. The *honji* of the *wakamiya* was Monju.

The status of the four deities of Kasuga reached such heights with the growth of Fujiwara political power that visits to the shrine by the emperor, retired emperor, and clan leaders were recorded almost daily in medieval chronicles. Indeed, even in the Heian period,

the reverence for this clan's *ujigami* was at such a peak that the Kasuga Shrine was elevated to national rank and was included among the twenty or so most important in the country. Moreover, branch shrines embodying the divine spirit of these Kasuga *kami* were established elsewhere in the territories held by the Kasuga Shrine and the Kōfuku-ji.

The *mandalas* produced in this environment were used principally in the Kōfuku-ji and affiliated temples, where they were hung on the occasion of important ceremonies in order to obtain the protection of the guardian deities they depicted. In Nara, popular religious societies that revered the Kasuga Shrine also collected and displayed such works during their ceremonies. *Mandalas* were made for other cults, such as

88. Kasuga Deer Mandala. *Colors on silk; ht 92.5 cm, w 39.6 cm. Muromachi period. Sekizan Zen-in, Kyoto.*

89. Kasuga Shrine Mandala. *Colors on silk; ht 108 cm, w 49 cm. 1300.*

90. Kasuga Shrine and Temple Mandala. *Kōfuku-ji, Nara.*

those of Sannō and Hachiman (see Chapters 6 and 7), and individuals had them made for personal devotion as well.

Deer Mandalas

Prominent in the imagery of the Kasuga cult—and, indeed, at the shrine itself—are the deer that roam freely by the hundreds through the Kasuga fields. The custom of sheltering the deer may derive from primitive ceremonies once held there, for it is thought that the early inhabitants of the area probably revered as intermediaries between gods and men the deer who wandered out from the sacred mountain. This idea is reflected in the *Kasuga Gongen Reigen Ki* (The Kasuga Gongen Miracles) and in the *Kōfuku-ji Yūrai Ki* (Origins of Kōfuku-ji), records which indicate that the origins of the deer *mandalas* lie in the tale that the deity of Kashima rode on the back of a white deer when he transferred his earthly abode to the foot of Mount Mikasa. Many deer *mandalas,* such as the one in Plate 83, portray Takemikazuchi no Mikoto in this posture. Because the deity's spirit is thought to dwell in this creature, however, he is also represented symbolically in the form of a deer alone. One of the best examples of this type of purely Shintō composition is shown in Plate 81. The inclusion of a sacred mirror inscribed with Takemikazuchi no Mikoto's *honji* on the back of the deer gives the *mandalas* shown in Plates 84 and 88 a more marked Buddhist flavor.

91. Kasuga Honji Mandala. *Kamakura period. Tokyo National Museum.*

Shrine Mandalas

Shrine *mandalas,* because they often depict landscape and so evoke the reverence for nature that is the heart of Shintō, are generally the most beautiful and appealing of all Shintō paintings. *Mandalas* of the Kasuga cult, produced in great numbers from the thirteenth through the sixteenth centuries, represent in almost maplike form the moonlit Kasuga Shrines hidden amid the cryptomeria of Mount Mikasa. Despite the architectural detail, however, the overall impression is one of delicacy and fragility; it is the natural setting and the sense of divine mystery it evokes that dominates these compositions.

The painting of which a detail is produced in Plate 77 is said to illustrate the shrines before their devasta-

tion by fire in 1180. Although the curved projections from the rooftops are distinctive features of the Kasuga Shrines, the red fence and gate or *torii* surrounding the principal sanctuaries are found in most Shintō establishments. Above the shrines are the names of the *honji* of the four Kasuga deities inscribed in Siddham characters, one of the scripts used to write Sanskrit.

The majority of works of this type, such as the one in Plates 80 and 89 inscribed by Retired Emperor Kameyama in 1300, depict the layout of the Kasuga Shrine complex. In the painting reproduced in Plate 90, however, attention is focused equally on the adjacent Kōfuku-ji. It is comprised of two sections, one above with an overall view of the Shintō establishment, another below with a hierarchical arrangement of Buddhist deities representing the most important tem-

92. Kasuga Jizō Mandala. *Muro-machi period. Mitsui Collection.*

93. Kasuga Pure Land Mandala. *Kamakura period. Nōman-in, Nara.*

94. Kasuga Mandala. *Muromachi period. Atami Art Museum, Atami.*

ples of the Kōfuku-ji. This composition might well be called a Kasuga shrine and temple *mandala.*

Honji-Butsu Mandalas

Illustrative of the Buddhist-Shintō amalgamation is another type of Kasuga *mandala* in which both forms of a deity are depicted. Plate 91 is a simple *honji-butsu mandala* depicting the Buddhist forms of the four presiding *kami* and *wakamiya* of Kasuga Shrine. There are six figures within a large globe occupying the upper half of the painting in order to accommodate the two opinions concerning the *honji* of the deity in the Ichi no Miya, thought to be either Shaka Nyorai or Fukū-kenjaku Kannon.

At first glance, Plate 92 would appear to be a Bud-

dhist painting of the Bodhisattva Jizō. However, he is represented here in his role as *honji* of the third of the four Kasuga shrines, that of the ancestral god from Hiraoka, Ame no Koyane no Mikoto. Jizō Bosatsu, as he is known in Japan, vowed to deliver man from suffering and is believed to descend to hell to save the wicked; the special protector of children and sinners, he is generally dressed as a monk, with staff in one hand and magic jewel in the other. Faith in him as a savior was particularly strong in the Kamakura period due to the influence of the Jōdo or Pure Land teachings that man could attain Buddhahood by rebirth in the Pure Land of Amida. In the Kasuga cult too, faith in him as the *honji* of the third shrine led to the belief that the mountain of Kasuga had the configuration of the Pure Land on Mount Potalaka, a mythical Bud-

95. Kasuga Mandala. *Detail of Plate 94.*

dhist paradise where the Bodhisattva was thought to dwell. Since it was believed on the one hand that the Pure Land was on Mount Kasuga and on the other that hell was located beneath the Kasuga plains, Jizō was the object of intense popular devotion. Even today, there is a Valley of Hell on Mount Kasuga where groups of stone Buddhist figures continue to reflect the amalgamation of folk beliefs and cult to Kasuga that developed in the medieval period.

The *Kasuga Jōdo Mandala* shown in Plate 93 exemplifies the interrelationship of Shintō and Buddhist painting. It represents Jizō riding on a white cloud rising from the third shrine, leading a reborn soul toward Mount Kasuga, much like Buddhist paintings called *raigō-zu* in which Amida is depicted descending from heaven with his divine retinue to receive the be-

liever's soul. Its creation may have been inspired by the story in the *Kasuga Gongen Reigen Ki* about the monk Shōen, a disciple of Gedatsu Shōnin (also known as Jōkei, 1155–1213), who fell into the hell beneath the Kasuga plains and was saved by Jizō.

Composite Mandalas

There is a certain category of works that combine elements from different types of *mandalas* and might therefore be called "composite *mandalas*." One such is the *mandala* in Plate 94, in which all the components of a shrine *mandala* are shown in a summary and formalized manner. In addition, a deer is placed on the peak of Mount Mikasa, and the images of the *suijaku* and their *honji* are arranged in rows in the uppermost

96. *Scene of* bugaku *at Kasuga Shrine. Section of the* Kasuga Gongen Reigen Ki *handscroll. 1309. Imperial Household Collection.*

portion (Plate 95). Because this *mandala* fuses the features of several *mandalas* rather schematically, it may have been painted for didactic purposes.

The Kasuga Gongen Reigen Ki

The *Kasuga Gongen Reigen Ki* is a narrative picture scroll relating miraculous tales of the four main Kasuga deities. The most renowned version, that in twenty scrolls in the Imperial Household collection, dates from 1309. According to an inscription at the end of the set, it was executed at the request of Saionji Kinhira, a descendant of the Fujiwara clan, and illustrated by Takashina Takakane, a painter of the Tosa school; members of the clan wrote the text. Although dealing primarily with the Kasuga Gongen, it contains numer-

ous scenes of everyday life in Nara, and even imaginary events, such as dreams or the visions of a sick person, are handled with considerable realism.

The scene reproduced in Plate 96 from the seventh scroll depicts a *bugaku* performance, a traditional Shintō ceremonial dance with musical accompaniment, held at Kasuga for the benefit of its deities in accordance with a dream of the monk Hanken of Kōfuku-ji in 1217. The heavily clothed spectators are priests of the temple, and formally dressed musicians playing flutes and drums are visible beneath the roof to the right. The inscription on this work indicates that it was treasured even in the fourteenth century. Abbots of two of the Kōfuku-ji's subtemples and a priest of the Kasuga Shrine assumed the responsibility of ensuring that it did not leave the temple grounds. It is

97. Manifestation of Kasuga Myōjin. *Fujita Art Museum, Osaka.*

even said their supervision was so strict that men under
the age of forty were not allowed to view the painting.

Manifestations of Kasuga Myōjin

Shintō paintings frequently show the legendary
manifestations of deities on earth, and many were
painted according to the visions of devotees. The images of Amida emerging from clouds above Mount
Nachi (Plate 126), Sōgyō Hachiman (Plate 68), Seiryū
Gongen (Plate 69) and Komori Myōjin (Plates 72,
73, 75), although inspired by different cults, are all

representative of this tendency to depict well-known
deities in familiar settings. The painting of the Kasuga
Myōjin in Plate 97 is a fine example of its kind based
on a dream of Fujiwara Fuyuhira, chief minister of
Emperor Hanazono, in 1312. The vision of Kasuga
Myōjin dressed in formal black attire was recorded at
Fuyuhira's request by an artist of the Takakane atelier.
Seated in an imperial carriage in a garden brightened
by the red foliage of young maples, the god is shown
holding in his black sleeve the volume of poetry that,
in Fuyuhira's dream, he gave to the minister. Another
painting also inspired by a dream is that of Kasuga
Wakamiya, which is shown in Plate 82.

6

Art of the Hachiman Cult

It is said that of the one hundred and ten thousand shrines in Japan, more are dedicated to Hachiman than to any other deity; in fact, Hachiman's popularity is such that there is probably no village without a sanctuary to him. Yet the rise and spread of the Hachiman cult is a phenomenon almost without parallel in Shintō history. Unlike the principal objects of Shintō worship, such as Amaterasu Omikami, the tutelary deity of Mount Hiei, or the *kami* of the Kasuga cult, all of which are mentioned in the *Kojiki* or *Nihon Shoki,* Hachiman seems to have developed outside the traditional Shintō sphere.

The Origins of the Cult

Although the beginnings of this cult are still the subject of extensive study, Hachiman seems to have been initially revered in northern Kyūshū, where it is said he manifested himself on a sacred site at the peak of Mount Maki in the Usa district of Buzen Province (modern Oita Prefecture). A small shrine later built at the foot of this mountain developed into the present-day Usa Hachiman Shrine, the birthplace of the Hachiman cult. Prayers were addressed to him as either a tutelary deity of one of the ancient clans in the Usa area or a regional agricultural god. Since the name Hachiman can also be read in Japanese as Yahata or Yawata, some scholars are of the opinion that he may have been the special guardian of the Hata, a clan of Chinese immigrants who lived in northern Kyūshū in ancient times. Others believe that *hata*, which can mean field, links him to ancient agricultural rites.

99. Wakamiya Hachiman. *Detail. Colors on silk; ht 78.2 cm, w 39.1 cm. Kamakura period. Hakkaku-in, Kyoto.*

98. Wakamiya Hachiman. *Late Kamakura period.*

The spread of devotion to Hachiman is probably due to his role as the guardian of clans associated with copper mining in the Usa region. Because the casting of the Great Buddha of Tōdai-ji caused a great shortage of metal in the eighth century, an emissary was sent to Hachiman at Usa to inquire where more might be found. When in accordance with his oracle gold was later found in the area of modern Aomori, Hachiman was introduced into the capital as the special guardian of the Tōdai-ji. As the first manifestation of the Shintō-Buddhist amalgamation in actual shrine building, this was a momentous event.

The penetration of the cult into the Yamato region in the eighth century has also been attributed to the fact that Hachiman, originally regarded as a guardian against epidemics, was called to Nara to quell both social unrest and illness. This aspect of Hachiman may have contributed to his great following among the masses throughout the country. Indeed, even today his shrines at Usa, at Iwashimizu near Kyoto, and at Kamakura are among the most frequented in Japan.

Hachiman's affiliation with the Tōdai-ji led to the name by which he was addressed from Heian times—Hachiman Daibosatsu or Great Bodhisattva Hachiman. The ninth-century portrayals of him in the guise of a monk, among the earliest extant examples of Shintō sculpture (see Chapter 3), further point to his role as precursor of the fusion of Shintō and Buddhism characteristic of later times.

A further development of the Hachiman cult led to

◁ *100. Hachiman in the guise of a monk (Sō-gyō Hachiman). Colors on silk; ht 148.2 cm, w 118.2 cm. Kamakura period. Jingō-ji, Kyoto.*

101. (left) Iwashimizu Hachiman Shrine Mandala. *Late Kamakura period. Rikkyoku-an, Kyoto.*

102. (right) Iwashimizu Hachiman Shrine Mandala. *Late Kamakura period. Inoue Collection.*

an emphasis on his role as a war god, and numerous shrines were established to protect cities and even the nation. The Iwashimizu Shrine, for example, was built southwest of the ancient capital of Kyoto precisely for this reason. Moreover, the powerful Minamoto clan adopted him as their tutelary deity in this role and enshrined him in the Tsurugaoka Hachiman Shrine in Kamakura.

Portrayals of Hachiman

Another dimension in the complex history of this deity is added by the inclusion of two female *kami* in early portrayals of him. Hachiman had also come to be regarded as a manifestation of Emperor Ojin, who is traditionally said to have reigned from 270 to 310. This attribution is the basis for the appearance of Ojin's mother, Empress Jingū, and his principal consort, Na-katsu-hime, in representations of the god. In the oldest portrayals of this triad, the sculptures in the Yakushi-ji (Plates 40, 41, 42) and Tō-ji (Plates 43, 47, 48), Hachi-man is depicted in the guise of a monk (Sōgyō Hachi-man), although the goddesses at his side wear the T'ang-style robes popular at the Heian court. (For a detailed discussion of these sculptures, see Chapter 3.)

Paintings of Hachiman strongly reflect the influence of Buddhism and especially that of the Esoteric Shin-gon sect, for Kōbō Daishi, its founder, revered him with special zeal. Like Buddhist works, images of the god were executed in accordance with the particular

104. The Iwashimizu Shrine. Detail of the Ippen Shōnin Eden *(Pictorial Biography of the Monk Ippen), by En'i Hōgen. Long handscroll on silk. 1299. Kankikō-ji, Kyoto.*

◁ *103.* Hachiman Suijaku Mandala. *Colors on silk; ht 79 cm, w 40 cm. Kamakura period. Raigō-ji, Osaka.*

conventions for facial expression, symbolic implements, hair style, type of dress and pattern, and overall coloring.

A ninth-century painting made at the request of Kōbō Daishi for the newly built Jingō-ji, a Shingon temple to the north of Kyoto, is the oldest of its kind on record. A Kamakura-period copy, reproduced in Plate 100, is still kept in the temple. The seated Hachiman is dressed in a monk's robe with a pattern of distant mountains, a monk's staff and rosary in hand. The red globe of the sun appears directly above his shaven head. The conventions observed in this work were followed in many later ones, most notably in a thirteenth-century statue by the Buddhist sculptor Kaikei (Plate 57), a National Treasure kept in the Hachiman Shrine of the Tōdai-ji. This piece is interesting evidence

that the Kei school of sculptors, of which Kaikei was a prominent member, had ties with the Shintō tradition even though it is especially renowned for Buddhist images.

Portrayals of Hachiman surrounded by several goddesses and child deities (*dōji*) are called Hachiman *suijaku mandalas.* The painting shown in Plate 103 is badly damaged in parts, but the remaining portions reveal a firm sense of line and vivid coloring. Hachiman is seated on a chair flanked by two goddesses, probably Empress Jingū and Nakatsu-hime. Another goddess, a child deity, and two black-robed attendants are depicted before him, thus representing each of the seven sanctuaries of the Hachiman Shrine at Iwashimizu. The seven Siddham letters arranged within circles above the figures also symbolize the names of these

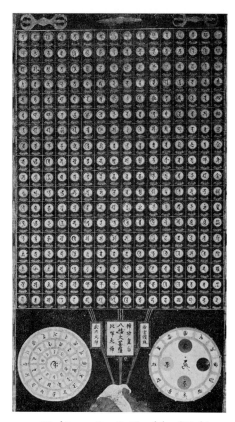

105. Hachiman Bonji Mandala *(Hachiman* mandala *with Siddham characters). Kamakura period.*

shrines. This *mandala* was probably made to be hung before images of Shintō deities or their *honji* on ceremonial occasions.

Shrine Mandalas and Related Works

Shrine *mandalas* depicting Shintō sanctuaries and their sacred parks were produced for the Hachiman cult as well as for other major cults, such as those of Kasuga (Chapter 5), Sannō (Chapter 7), and Kumano (Chapter 8). Most renowned of the Hachiman *mandalas* are those with scenes of the Iwashimizu Hachiman Shrine. This Hachiman shrine is said to have been founded in 859 by the monk Gyōkyō of the Daian-ji temple, and the appearance of its sanctuaries has not changed much to this day. The shrine was originally comprised of sanctuaries, each with ritual significance, on the upper and lower parts of Otokoyama mountain. In the Kamakura period, however, they were fused into a single complex.

Portrayals of the Iwashimizu shrine are of two types: The earlier style presents an overall view of the shrine compound, including its subordinate shrines and associated Buddhist structures; later artists preferred to paint the shrine from a different perspective. The *mandala* in Plate 85 is of the former type, and the realism with which the arrangement and construction of the buildings is shown gives it great value as an architectural and historical record. Plate 101 shows an Iwashimizu shrine *mandala* of the second type preserved in the Rikkyoku-an of the Tōfuku-ji monastery in Kyoto. Although small, it is a bold composition pre-

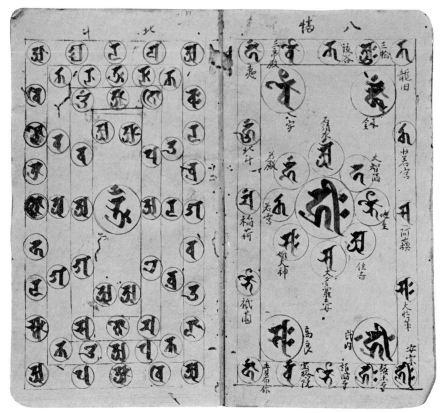

106. Hachiman Bonji Mandala *(Hachiman* mandala *with Siddham characters). Late six-teenth century. Ninna-ji, Kyoto.*

senting an aerial view of the shrine and is marked by a fine sense of color. The plan of the painting in Plate 102 is almost identical except for the addition of images of the *honji-butsu* of the *kami* of the seven Hachiman sanctuaries at Iwashimizu. Another view of the shrine precincts is shown in Plate 104, in a portion of the narrative scroll describing the journeys of the monk Ippen.

The unusual *mandala* reproduced in Plate 105 is a striking example of the Hachiman cult's intimate relationship with Esoteric Buddhism. It is a representation of a *dhāraṇī* or magic formula written in elegant Sid-

dham letters, each atop a lotus flower. In the foreground are two jeweled wheels within which more Siddham characters are arranged, and between them is a rock bearing a robe with a distant mountain pattern symbolizing Hachiman. The rays emitted from the rock represent the Hachiman triad, Hachiman Waka-miya, and Takeshi-uchi Okami. A more diagrammatic work also comprised of Siddham letters appears in Plate 106, which shows a page from a compilation of thirty-five types of Buddhist-Shintō *mandalas* executed in the Kōji era (1555–58). (The Sannō *mandala* in Plate 120 is another example from the same book.)

7

Art of the Sannō Cult

Mount Hiei north of Kyoto is known primarily as the center of the Tendai sect in Japan founded by Dengyō Daishi (767–822) in the early ninth century, but it is also the birthplace of a much older cult to the Shintō tutelary deity of the mountain, Sannō or Mountain King. In fact, when Dengyō Daishi selected Mount Hiei as the site of his sect, he addressed prayers to Sannō to ensure the god's approval and protection of the new religious center. This is the basis for the close relationship between the Sannō cult and the Tendai sect.

The Twenty-one Sannō Shrines

The religious establishment devoted to this *kami,* located at the eastern foot of Mount Hiei overlooking Lake Biwa, is called the Hie (or Hiyoshi) Shrine and is divided into two sections. The Eastern Shrine embodies Oyamagui no Mikoto, the tutelary deity of the mountain, while the Western Shrine embodies Inamuchi no Mikoto, originally from Mount Miwa in Nara Prefecture. These two sanctuaries, together with five others associated with them, are called collectively the Seven Upper Sannō Shrines and comprise the core of the Sannō cult. There are, however, also groups of Seven Middle Sannō Shrines and Seven Lower Sannō Shrines, bringing the total number to twenty-one. Moreover, during the Kamakura period, numerous subshrines and Buddhist temples were added, creating a vast religious complex extending over the entire mountain and called the One Hundred and Eight Inner and One Hundred and Eight Outer

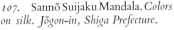

107. Sannō Suijaku Mandala. *Colors on silk. Jōgon-in, Shiga Prefecture.*

108. Sannō Suijaku Mandala. *Gaku-en-ji, Shimane Prefecture.*

Shrines. These designations, so cumbersome to Western readers, are commonly encountered in Buddhist contexts, and in fact, both the numbers seven and one hundred and eight are of special Buddhist significance: The former is associated with Tendai teachings regarding the Seven Constellations, while the latter is, according to most sects, the number of spiritual impediments.

The *mandalas* associated with this cult generally focus on the Seven Upper Sannō Shrines whose *kami* and their Buddhist counterparts are presented in Plate 109. The first four shrines are associated with the Eastern Shrine; the latter three are associated with the Western Shrine.

One of the characteristics of Shintō metaphysics is that the spirit or *mitama* of a *kami* is thought to be com-

posed of several parts, the two principal being the *aramitama* or "rough spirit," and *nigimitama* or "pacific spirit." Consequently, the parts of the *mitama* of a deity can be enshrined in more than one shrine. As can be seen in the listing in Plate 109, this is true of Oyamagui no Mikoto, whose *nigimitama* is in the Eastern Shrine, while his *aramitama* is in the Ushiōgū. The belief that a divine spirit could be divided into numerous parts is also the basis for the establishment of new shrines in other localities devoted to the same deity, and explains the existence of Hie shrines throughout the country, most notably in Tokyo.

Most Shintō *mandalas*, whether of the *suijaku, honji-butsu* or shrine types, were used in a similar manner. Like the Kasuga *mandalas* discussed in Chapter 5, they were displayed during important rites in Buddhist

SHRINE	OLD NAME	SITE	KAMI	HONJI
Eastern	Ni no Miya	Foot	Oyamagui no Mikoto (*nigimitama*)	Yakushi Nyorai
Jukegū	Jūzenji	Foot	Tamayori-hime no Mikoto (*nigimitama*)	Jizō Bosatsu
Ushiōgū	Hachiōji	Peak	Oyamagui no Mikoto (*aramitama*)	Senju Kannon
San no Miya	San no Miya	Peak	Tamayori-hime no Mikoto (*aramitama*)	Fugen Bosatsu
Western	Omiya	Foot	Onamuchi no Mikoto	Shaka Nyorai
Usa no Miya	Shoshinji	Foot	Tagori-hime no Mikoto	Amida Nyorai
Shirayamagū	Marōdo	Foot	Shirayama-hime no Mikoto	Jūichimen Kannon

109. Deities of the Seven Upper Sannō Shrines.

temples of the sect with which they were affiliated in order to ensure protection by the *kami* they portrayed. However, Sannō *mandalas* were also exhibited as the principal devotional images for special ceremonies held from time to time in Tendai temples. The Sannō cult was widespread among the populace living around Mount Hiei, and the religious brotherhoods that were formed also collected and displayed old Sannō *mandalas* as images of special reverence.

Suijaku Mandalas

A Sannō *mandala* portraying the *kami* in the Seven Upper Shrines in their *suijaku* forms at the entrance of a sanctuary is shown in Plate 107. Some of the deities

of the Seven Central Shrines are also shown. The three most highly revered gods of the Western, Eastern, and Usa no Miya shrines appear in the guise of monks seated on platforms in the center of the composition. The male and female deities in the upper right- and left-hand corners are enshrined in the subshrines of the Eastern Shrine. Below the principal triad are the *kami* in the two remaining Upper Sannō Shrines—Jūzenji Gongen as a priest (in the Jukegū) and Marōdo Gongen (in the Shirayamagū). In the lower portion of the painting are some of the gods of the Central Sannō Shrines, most notably a peculiar monkey-faced figure in formal hat and gown.

Indicative of the close affiliation with the Tendai sect are the portrayals in the foreground of Dengyō

110. Sannō Honji-Butsu Mandala. *Colors on silk; ht 45 cm, w 30 cm. Enryaku-ji, Shiga Prefecture.*

Daishi with two other abbots of Enryaku-ji—Jikaku Daishi, also known as Ennin and famous for his pilgrimage to China in the mid-ninth century, and Ganzan Daishi, the object of a popular cult in his own right. The inclusion of important figures in the Buddhist tradition is not unique to Sannō *mandalas,* for a work inspired by the Kumano cult (Plate 130) also depicts Chishō Daishi (814–91), founder of the Jimon branch of the Tendai sect and closely affiliated with Kumano.

Although Omiya Gongen of the Western Shrine appears as a monk in this painting (Plate 107), he can also be depicted as a court figure wearing T'ang-style robes and cap, because there are two traditions concerning his *suijaku* form. The same is true of his *honji.*

This portrayal of him is of particular interest, since works in which he appears in his *suijaku* form are rare.

Honji Mandalas

Three examples of Sannō *honji mandalas* are shown in Plates 110, 111, and 119. The work in Plate 111, formerly preserved in the Kannon-ji in Shiga, depicts the Buddhas and Bodhisattvas seated on platforms in front of screens at what appears to be the entrance of a shrine—much the same arrangement used in the *suijaku mandala* shown in Plate 107. Shaka, Yakushi, and Amida Nyorai, the *honji* of the three principal Sannō deities, appear in the center; above them are Senju Kannon flanked by Jūichimen Kannon and Fugen Bo-

111. Sannō Honji-Butsu Mandala. *Colors on silk; ht 92.3 cm, w 46 cm.*

112. Sannō Shrine Mandala. *Colors on silk; ht 118.8 cm, w 76.7 cm. Late Kamakura period. Hyakusai-ji, Shiga Prefecture.*

113. Sannō Shrine Mandala. *Colors on silk; ht 120 cm, w 60 cm. Dominating this mandala is the sacred Mount* ▷
Hachiōji, and at its foot is the Sannō shrine complex, giving a clear picture of architectural style and shrine layout in
the medieval period. As was the case with many others made at this time, this mandala was also meant to be an object of
worship. In three rows across the top are the twenty-one Sannō deities, represented first in Siddham characters, followed
by their portraits as Buddhist honji and then as Shintō kami. Early Muromachi period.

114. Secret Sannō Mandala. *Hie Shrine, Shiga Prefecture.*

satsu; and below is Jizō Bosatsu, corresponding to the remaining four upper shrines. The three circles inscribed with Siddham characters in the upper section of the composition represent the *honji-butsu* of all twenty-one shrines. Fudō Myō-ō and Bishamon-ten, both associated with the Seven Central Sannō Shrines, serve as guardians.

The oldest extant Sannō *honji mandala* may be the one in the Enryaku-ji on Mount Hiei illustrated in Plate 110. Although this work is less elaborate than that in Plate 111 and the deities differ somewhat in appearance, iconographically it is identical. It is rather small in size, but is marked by the fine gold leaf used to highlight the figures. Plate 119 shows a rare *honji-butsu mandala* painted on the wooden panels of a portable

shrine. The *honji* of the Seven Upper Shrines and around them those of four other shrines are arranged on the central front panel; six *kami* are depicted on the open side panels (Plate 118 shows a diagram of their disposition).

Shrine Mandalas

The extensive Hie Shrine compound lies below the peaks of Mount Hiei and is encircled by the sacred Mount Hachiōji. Its cinnabar-colored sanctuaries, several of which have been designated National Treasures or Important Cultural Properties, blend harmoniously with the luxuriant green of the ancient cryptomeria in the vicinity. Groups of old tombs, the sacred trees, the

115. Sannō Shrine Mandala. *Colors on silk; ht 115 cm, w 54.8 cm. Kamakura period. Reiun-ji, Tokyo.*

116. Sannō Treasure Pagoda Mandala *(Sannō Hōtō Mandara). Kanda Collection.*

117. Sannō Bonji Mandala *(Sannō* mandala *with Siddham characters). Yamamoto Collection.*

pure streams and natural springs all preserve the original ambiance of the Hie cult in remote antiquity. But the intermingling of medieval and modern beliefs adds to the diversity of its history, ritual practices, offerings, and dances.

Sannō shrine *mandalas* convey the spirit of the cult as well as recall the actual appearance of the shrines and gardens. The painting reproduced in Plate 112, for instance, depicts a vast panorama of all twenty-one shrines from the sacred mountain to the river. There are large images of the *honji-butsu* of the Seven Upper Sannō Shrines at the site of each sanctuary, and several subordinate shrines are represented by their deities in *suijaku* form.

An impressive shrine *mandala* dominated by Hachi-

ōji with shrines clustered at its foot is illustrated in Plate 113. This work is useful for architectural history, since both the shrines and the Buddhist establishments are depicted as they were in medieval times. The *Secret Sannō Mandala* shown in Plate 114 records the appearance of the shrines in the late sixteenth century as they were reconstructed after a fire. The special designation "secret" *(himitsu)* is said to derive from the practice of contemplating such works as if one were actually making a pilgrimage to the shrine.

Plate 123, a detail from another Sannō *mandala*, clearly reveals the meticulous attention to shrine architecture characteristic of this type of painting. Since this *mandala* was intended as an object of devotion rather than an architectural record, it also shows the *honji-butsu* of

Karasu Tengu Goin	*Kehi* Seishi BS		*Seijō* Nyoirin K	*Ushimiko* Daitoku Myō-ō
	San no Miya Fugen BS		*Hachiōji* Senju K	
Shingyōji Kichijō-ten	*Shōshinji* Amida	*Omiya* Shaka	*Ni no Miya* Yakushi	*Shōzenji* Ryūjū BS
	Marōdo Jūichimen K		*Jūzenji* Jizō BS	
Gyōji Bishamon-ten	*Oji* Monju BS		*Shimo Hachiōji* Kokūzō BS	*Hayao* Fudō Myō-ō

118. *Schematic diagram of the deities of Sannō shown in Plate 119. Forms not illustrated are shown in italic; the abbreviations BS and K indicate Bodhisattva (Bosatsu) and Kannon, respectively.*

each shrine. The inclusion of *kakebotoke,* metal plaques with Buddhist figures in relief, in front of each sanctuary; of pairs of lion-dogs or *koma-inu* on the veranda surrounding each shrine; and even of monkeys, indigenous to Mount Hiei, helps convey the appearance of the shrine in the middle ages.

Other Paintings

Mandalas of pagodas within which Buddhas are seated are common in the Buddhist tradition, but less so in Shintō art. One example is the *Sannō Treasure Pagoda Mandala* shown in Plate 116. Until its destruction by fire in the Genki era (1570–73) uprisings, a circular pagoda with a four-cornered roof or "treasure pagoda" *(hōtō)* stood in the Hie Shrine compound together with numerous other Buddhist structures. This is the pagoda illustrated in the painting. It is situated below Mount Hiei and overlooks the sandbar-shaped Lake Biwa. Even the well-known Karasaki Pine Tree in the center of the lake is included. Inside the building is Dainichi Nyorai; in the four corners are the kings of the four directions.

Two *mandalas* with strong Buddhist flavor are reproduced in Plates 117 and 120. Both are comprised of Siddham letters representing the *honji* of the principal deities of the Sannō cult. Plate 120 shows a page of a book from which another page is illustrated in Plate 106.

The Sannō Festival was traditionally held on the

119.   Sannō Honji Mandala. *Ht 97 cm, w 57.8 cm. This unusual work, painted on the inside panels of a miniature shrine, includes the* seventeen honji *of the Sannō shrines, each drawn with iconographic exactitude and a fine sense of line and color. The images are painted on silk cloth glued to the box, over which gold foil has been applied. (See Plate 118 for a diagram of the deities.) Kamakura period. Nezu Art Museum, Tokyo.*

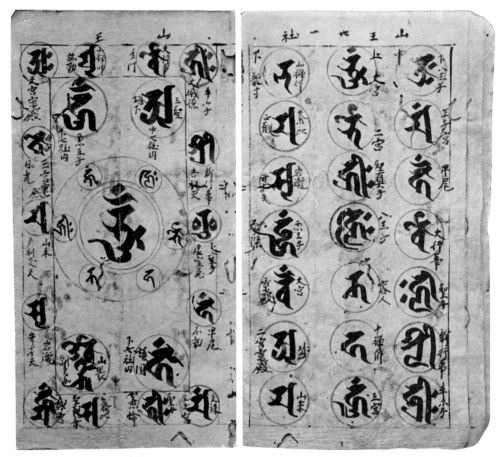

120. Sannō Bonji Mandala *(Sannō* mandala *with Siddham characters). Late sixteenth century.* Ninna-ji, Kyoto.

days before and after the Day of the Monkey in the fourth lunar month; it has now been fixed on April 12 to 15. The festivals on the first two days, the Day of the Horse and the Day of the Sheep, observe the important Shintō custom of renewing the life of the *kami (mi-are).* The festival of the Day of the Monkey was initially associated only with the Western Shrine and its subshrines, but later came to involve all seven shrines. Gay and lavish, this spectacle has been the sub-

ject of many screen paintings. Plate 121, for example, shows a portion of the oldest extant Sannō festival screen; it depicts the events of the Day of the Monkey, the liveliest of the three. *Mikoshi* (portable shrines) are being transported across Lake Biwa to the Karasaki Pine Tree, around which groups of noisy spectators, including the belligerent armed monks of Mount Hiei, are clustered in small boats.

121. Sannō Festival Screen. *Detail. Momoyama period. Dannō Hōrin-ji, Kyoto.*

(overleaf)

122. Hachiman Wakamiya Dōji. *Colors on silk; ht 30 cm, w 21 cm. This is one of the many portrayals of deities as children (dōji)* ▷ *whose youthful, fresh looks were inspired by the Shintō concept of rejuvenation and rebirth. His noble yet doll-like features would seem to be the work of an artist trained in Kyoto. Rikkyoku-an, Kyoto.*

123. Sannō Shrine Mandala. *Detail. Colors on silk; ht 97 cm, w 64.2 cm. Although intended as a devotional painting, this work is* ▷ *an excellent source of information about the architecture and atmosphere of the Hie Shrine in the medieval period. The mandala shows the Seven Sannō Shrines along with subordinate shrines, each with its deity's Buddhist honji in a large golden globe. Votive plaques (kake-botoke) hang from the eaves, and a pair of koma-inu flank each entry. The monkeys sacred to Mount Hiei are visible about the shrines. Yamato Bunkakan, Nara.*

8

Art of the Kumano Cult

On the southern part of the Kii Peninsula in Waka- yama Prefecture, there are three shrines of great sanctity called the Hongū, Shingū, and Nachi, and known collectively as the Kumano Three Mountains (Kumano Sanzan). Ketsumiko, identified with Susano- o no Mikoto, the impetuous brother of the sun god- dess who taught the world shipbuilding and forestry, is enshrined in the Hongū or Kumano ni Masu Shrine, while Hayatama no Okami dwells in the Shingū or Hayatama Shrine. Fusumi no Okami, generally thought to be Hayatama's female consort, is in the Nachi Shrine.

The Origins of the Cult

The origins of the three shrines are obscure but can certainly be linked to the naturalistic folk cults of early

Japan. The belief that developed around both the Hon- gū and the Shingū, located at the mouth and upper stream of the Kumano River, was most likely asso- ciated with industry—forestry, transportation, and mining—in which the river played such an important role. The waterfall at Nachi, on the other hand, seems to have been revered primarily for its natural beauty. The union of these two groups of shrines was probably the result of Buddhist influence.

From Heian times, the Kumano cult was deeply overlaid with Buddhist overtones because of its asso- ciation with the Tendai sect, especially the Mii-dera branch centered in the temple of the same name on the shores of Lake Biwa near Kyoto. The rise of a sect of wandering ascetics called Shugendō, whose mem- bers generally go by the name *yamabushi* (those who sleep in the mountains) also played a considerable role

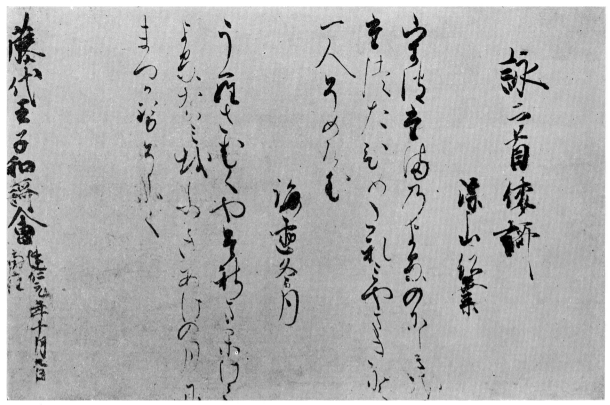

124.   Kumano Gaishi *(Record of Poetry Gathering along the Way to Kumano). Calligraphy by Jyakuren. 1201. Yōmei Library, Kyoto.*

in the shaping of the cult. This sect, which combines the doctrines of Esoteric Buddhism, Shintō, and Taoism, lays particular stress on ascetic practices in seclusion deep in the mountains in order to acquire magico-religious powers.

Mainly associated with the mountainous regions of Omine and Yoshino where En no Gyōja (b. 634), generally considered the sect's founder, first practiced, the movement soon spread to the three mountains of Kumano. Thus the religious spheres of the Kumano Sanzan (three mountains) and of Mount Kimpu, with its tutelary deity Zaō Gongen, came to be considered by members of this sect as a single holy region. One can get some idea of the vastness of the natural setting from Kumano *mandalas* such as the one reproduced in Plate 130, which includes the *kami* of Yoshino and Mount Kimpu.

The Kumano cult was also affected by the great religious movement of late Heian times that touched all Japanese spiritual life—the development of mass or popular Buddhism based on doctrines of faith rather than strong self-discipline. It coincided with the growth in popularity of the Buddha Amida, in whose Western Paradise or Pure Land the faithful, regardless of social standing or past deeds, might be reborn. An earthly paradise called Mount Potalaka was thought to be the dwelling of Amida's messenger, the compassionate Kannon, who was deeply committed to aiding mortals to attain salvation. The notion of Mount Potalaka had caught the imagination of the common people throughout East Asia, and they sought to find its precise location in areas they might visit or easily envision. In Japan the belief arose that this paradise was actually located at Kumano, in the vicinity of

125.   Saigyō Monogatari Emaki *(Biography of the Monk Saigyō). Detail of a handscroll depicting Saigyō writing a poem on the fence of the Yagami Oji Shrine on the road to Kumano, one of the ninety-nine such shrines along the pilgrimage road. Thirteenth century. Ohara Collection, Okayama Prefecture.*

126. Manifestation of Amida at Mount Nachi. *Colors on silk; ht 114.5 cm, w 51.5 cm. 1328. Dannō Hōrin-ji, Kyoto.*

127.   *The principal shrine of Kumano, from a section of the* Ippen Shōnin Eden *(Pictorial Biography of the Monk Ippen), by En'i Hōgen. In the summer of 1274, the monk Ippen made a pilgrimage to Kumano, where he received an oracle from the Kumano Gongen confirming him in his faith. Though a devotee of Amida, Ippen, like many other Buddhist monks, was drawn to the native religion. This pictorial biography, which records his visits to a number of Shintō centers, is a valuable record of Kamakura-period shrine architecture. Long handscroll on silk. Thirteenth century. Kankikō-ji, Kyoto.*

SHRINE	HONJI	SHINTŌ FORM
Hongū	Amida Nyorai	Monk
Shingū	Yakushi Nyorai	Layman
Nachi	Senju Kannon	Female
Wakamiya	Jūichimen Kannon	Female
Zenshi no Miya	Jizō Bosatsu	Monk/layman
Hijiri no Miya	Ryūju Bosatsu	Monk
Chigo no Miya	Nyoirin Kannon	Child deity
Komori no Miya	Shō Kannon	Female
Ichi-man Jū-man	Fugen/Monju Bosatsu	Layman
Kanjō Jūgosho	Shaka Nyorai	—
Hikō Yasha	Fudō Myō-ō	—
Komemochi Dōji	Bishamon-ten	—
Taki no Miya	Senju Kannon	—

128. The principal Kumano deities.

Nachi Falls. (However, as noted in Chapter 5, it was also thought to be at Kasuga in Nara.)

The awe-inspiring natural beauty of the region certainly contributed to the growth of these traditions, but Kumano's mountainous landscape and proximity to the sea—the former long associated with death and the latter with rebirth—were perhaps most instrumental in their development. It is therefore not surprising that both the Buddha Amida and Kannon appear prominently in paintings associated with the Kumano cult. The *Manifestation of Amida at Mount Nachi* in Plate 126 is a case in point. The painting is based on a tale about an old woman who over the years prayed forty-eight times that she might make a pilgrimage to Kumano. When at the age of seventy her wish was finally fulfilled and she neared the Miya Oji Shrine at Hama, Amida suddenly appeared enveloped in purple clouds high above Nachi Mountain. The date 1328 and the name of a monk of the Enkaku-ji temple in Kamakura are inscribed in the cartouche in the upper portion of the composition.

A number of individuals and religious groups contributed to the spread of the Kumano cult throughout Japan. Special guides, for example, explained the religious mysteries of Kumano; other spiritual leaders propagated the cult in the provinces; and wandering nuns traveled all over the country soliciting offerings for the shrine and singing songs in its praise. Ippen Shōnin (1239–89), a monk devoted to the savior Amida, made a pilgrimage to Kumano, where in a great vision he found confirmation of the rightness of his faith. Twelve narrative scrolls called the *Ippen Shōnin Eden,* painted

129. Kumano Honji Mandala. *Colors on silk; ht 83.3 cm, w 40.9 cm. Kamakura period. Tosen Shrine, Hyōgo Prefecture.*

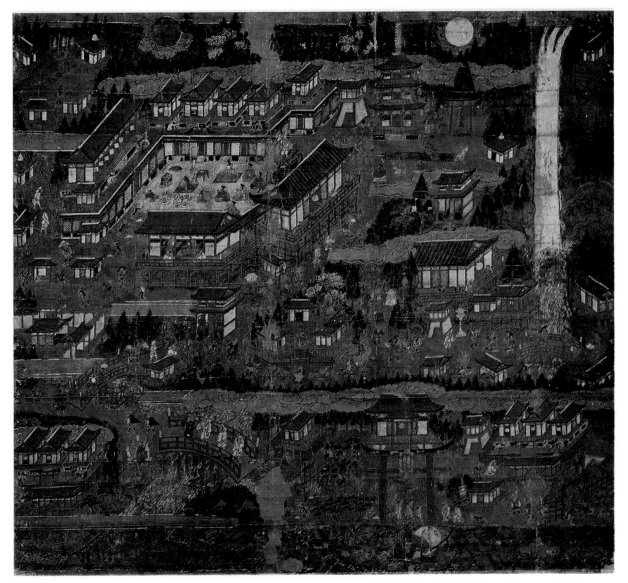

131.   Kumano Nachi Shrine Pilgrimage Mandala. *Colors on silk; ht 152 cm, w 165 cm. In this* mandala, *the artist has deftly combined the setting of the Nachi Shrine, various legends of the Kumano cult, and scenes of a pilgrimage. Below the sun and moon are the principal sanctuary, subsidiary shrines, and affiliated Buddhist temples; to the right is the Nachi waterfall. Below is the great torii of Kumano Nachi Gongen, and, in the sea, a scene of a crossing to Mount Potalaka, believed to be located at Nachi. In the courtyard of the principal shrine the retired emperor Goshirakawa is attending a service, and beneath the falls, a monk is being rescued by a deity. Momoyama period. Tōkei Shrine, Wakayama Prefecture.*

◁   130.   Kumano Honji Mandala. *Detail. Colors on silk; ht 146 cm, w 51.4 cm. The honji of the twelve Kumano gods are depicted in the center of the painting against a blue background, while the Eleven-headed Thousand-armed Kannon, the* honji *of Nachi Falls, and the Heian-period monk Chishō Daishi are shown to the right. Mount Omine, presided over by Zaō Gongen and his attendants, is represented in the upper portion, and the ninety-nine Oji Shrines in the lower portion, in a condensation of the landscape settings of various cults from Kumano on Kii Peninsula to Mount Hiei in Shiga Prefecture. Kamakura period. Shōgo-in, Kyoto.*

132. Kumano Sanzan Shrine Mandala. *Cleveland Museum of Art.*

133. Kumano Honji-Butsu Mandala. *Kamakura period. Kōzan-ji, Kyoto.*

in 1299 by a close follower, commemorate his travels all over the country. A section from the third scroll reproduced in Plate 127 illustrates the Hongū at Kumano and the many pilgrims gathered there. Ippen is shown twice in dark robes in the forecourt.

One of the most interesting developments associated with Kumano is the faith in a type of paper sanctified there by printing on it an image of a large crow named Yatagarasu. According to Shintō mythology, this bird was a divine messenger who guided the emperor Jimmu through this mountainous region. The holy paper, called Kumano Gō-ō, was used frequently throughout Japan for legal documents.

Treasured for their calligraphic beauty are the records of poetry meetings held by monk-emperors and noblemen at the Oji Shrines, resting places along the pilgrimage route. Emperor Gotoba (r. 1184–98), for instance, who over a period of twenty-four years made twenty-eight pilgrimages to Kumano, would often rest at one of the Oji Shrines. Gathering together his attendants, he would sit with them and recite and compose poetry, which would then be beautifully written in the calligraphic style of the time. Many retired emperors and renowned calligraphers, such as Fujiwara no Masatsune, Fujiwara no Teika, and the monk Jyakuren, have left such *Kumano Gaishi.* The sample reproduced in Plate 124 was composed by Jyakuren while on a pilgrimage to Kumano in the winter of 1201 in the company of Emperor Gotoba. Both this piece and a matching one written by the emperor are characterized by a somewhat viscous, wet style that replaced the elegant femininity of Heian calligraphy.

134.   Kumano shrine mandala with the Kumano and Nachi deities. Kamakura period. Shōgo-in, Kyoto.

The Pilgrimage to Kumano

From the tenth century onward, the cult of Kumano was widespread at all levels of society; even the imperial family began to make frequent pilgrimages. The prestige of the shrines was greatly enhanced by the visits of Retired Emperor Uda in 907, the Monk-Emperor Kazan (r. 984–986), who went there three times a year, and Emperor Shirakawa (r. 1072–86), who visited Kumano twelve times. Subsequently, Emperor Toba (r. 1107–23) and Retired Emperors Gotoba and Goshirakawa paid twenty-three, twenty-eight, and thirty-three visits, respectively.

Imperial pilgrimages were no light matter. Approximately two hundred miles separated the capital in Kyoto from the principal shrine of Kumano; adding eighty miles—the distance of the pilgrimage between the three shrines—the round trip came to more than five hundred miles. The average journey of an imperial family required about twenty days in all, and one can easily imagine the expense, complexity, and protocol involved. Prior to departure, the emperor had to perform ablutions in seclusion in a hut reserved for this purpose. At the numerous shrines along the way, gatherings for composing thirty-one syllable poems or *waka* were customarily held; in addition, prayers, offerings, and scripture readings were expected at the three Kumano Shrines. Shrine priests, Buddhist monks, and special guides who explained religious matters to the pilgrim were presented with suitable gifts on days of religious significance.

From Kyoto, after leaving the Toba Purification

135. Kumano Honji-Butsu Mandala. *Saikyō-ji, Shiga Prefecture.*

Hut, the pilgrim boarded a river boat. Then from the shore of the Tenjin Bridge at Osaka, farther to the south, he took the overland route along the Nankai Highway that led to the Kumano Road, whose first landmark was the Kubotsu Oji Shrine at Settsu. There were ninety-nine (today ninety-five) of these so-called Oji Shrines along the Kumano Road at a distance of approximately a mile from each other, and by following them one reached the Kumano Sanzan. Because of the widespread popular belief it inspired, the streams of travelers who thronged this devotional route day and night came to be compared to a column of ants. We can get some idea of the source of inspiration for such trips from an oracle recorded in the *Kumano Engi* (Legends of Kumano). Addressing himself to the populaces of the sixty-odd provinces of

Japan, the deity of each of the three shrines promises peace and prosperity in this life and assures rebirth in paradise should one make a pilgrimage to his shrine. At least one visit to Kumano during one's lifetime was therefore deemed essential to one's well-being in this world and the next.

Along the Kumano Road

Although the traveler along the Kumano Road cannot fail to be struck by its natural beauty, the appeal of Kumano and its cult lies more in the intimate relationship between the spirit of nature and religion. A poem contained in the *Ryōjin Hishō,* a late Heian compilation, evokes this interaction between the inner and outer world fundamental to the mood of Kumano in

136.   Shugendō pilgrim. Detail of Plate 135.

its references to the "road of compassion" and to the routes from the southwest (the Kii Road) and northeast (Ise Road) leading to the shrines:

> On the pilgrimage to Kumano
> From the Kii or Ise Road
> Be you near or far,
> If you follow the road of compassion,
> Neither the Kii nor the Ise Road
> Is distant.

The great falls that pour forth from the face of Mount Nachi into a deep pool whose pure spring waters flow bubbling and foaming far into the sea at the Kumano Channel certainly evokes this fusion of nature and divine forces. When one sees its mysterious waters gleaming in the moonlight, it is easy to under-

stand how it came to be revered as a deity. At its mouth once stood a temple named Enjō-ji, built by the devout emperor Kazan in the tenth century. Only its name remains, carved on a moss-covered stone wall hidden amid luxuriant shrubbery, but the ambiance of that time lingers on in the rumble of the waterfall and the whispering of the pines.

Farther along the route, in the vicinity of the Hatsu-shimmon Oji Shrine, are mountain hot springs where today, as in the past, weary travelers pass the night in rustic inns and refresh themselves by bathing in the soothing waters. Thus they prepare for the following day's trip down the Kumano River, when they will pay calls at the Hayatama and Nachi shrines on the way to the Hongū.

Although ninety-nine Oji Shrines once marked the

way of the pilgrim along the Kumano Road, today only their ruins—extending from the Kubotsu Oji Shrine in Settsu to the Tafuke Oji Shrine in Nachi—testify to the popularity of this pilgrimage route. The traces of these shrines are generally no more than stone signposts in the shade of a single cryptomeria, stone pagodas, or fragments of stone lanterns. Even with the aid of a map, they are difficult to locate.

If one makes a special stop beyond the Misu Pass, between the Misuzu Oji and the Inabane Oji shrines, one can still see the Yagami Oji, a small shrine along what was the road used by the imperial cortege. This is the shrine commemorated in the thirteenth-century *Saigyō Monogatari Emaki* (Biography of the Monk Saigyō), of which a detail is reproduced in Plate 125. The scene from the second of the two extant scrolls depicts Saigyō, formerly a warrior in the imperial service, before the Yagami Oji Shrine. Deeply moved by the sight of blossoming cherry trees in the spring snow, he composed a poem and wrote it on the sacred red fence outside the sanctuary.

> The long-awaited
> Cherry trees of Yagami
> Have come to bloom,
> Blow not fiercely down the slopes,
> O winds of Misu Mountain.

This image of the solitary black-robed monk kneeling before the brightly colored fence surrounded by swaying pines is handled with both a refined sense of realism and an awareness of the *yamato-e* painting tradition. It is said that in Edo times (1603–1868), villagers gathered to worship the resident *kami* of this small plot, but even today, the large shrine compound enclosed by a dense copse of trees retains the atmosphere of those remote days.

Kumano Mandalas

There are altogether twelve *kami* at Kumano who figure in *mandalas* and generally go by the name Twelve Kumano Gongen. Occasionally, however, the deity of Nachi Falls is included, thus increasing their

137. Kumano Suijaku Mandala. *Colors on silk; ht 100 cm, w 40 cm. Seikadō Foundation, Tokyo.*

number to thirteen. Three of these are, of course, the main gods of the Hongū, Shingū, and Nachi shrines, known collectively as the Three Kumano Gongen. The others are enshrined in the nine remaining principal shrines of Kumano. The names of the twelve (or thirteen) shrines, the appearance of each deity, and his corresponding *honji* form are shown in the listing in Plate 128.

Plate 133 shows a Kumano *honji-butsu mandala* representing the principal deities of the Kumano Sanzan with Amida (of the Hongū) in the center, Yakushi Nyorai (Shingū) to the right, and the Eleven-headed Thousand-armed Kannon (Nachi) to the left. Directly below the central figure is Jūichimen Kannon (Wakamiya) with Jizō Bosatsu (Zenshi no Miya) and Ryūju Bosatsu (Hijiri no Miya) to the left and right. Shaka Nyorai (Kanjō Jūgosho) is just above Amida with Nyoirin Kannon (Chigo no Miya) and Shō Kannon (Komori no Miya) to each side. In the mountainous upper portion of the composition stand the enraged Zaō Gongen, the special guardian of the Shugendō sect, and his five child attendants—the deities of Mount Yoshino and Mount Kimpu—an indication of the ties between the Kumano cult and Shugendō. The many *honji* of the Oji Shrines are gathered at the base.

The *mandala* reproduced in Plate 130 is comprised in large measure of elements of landscape that add considerably to its appeal. Since it is associated with Nachi, both the waterfall and its Buddhist counterpart (the Eleven-headed Thousand-armed Kannon) are included. It is identical to the painting in Plate 133 in its arrangement of the various deities in the mountains and of those of the Oji Shrines, but its affiliation with the special cult that developed in the Mii-dera branch of the Tendai sect is evident in the depiction of the monk Chishō Daishi near the basin of the waterfall (lower right-hand corner).

A painting that recently came to light at the Saikyō-ji in Shiga Prefecture depicting the *honji* of the twelve *gongen* before a shrine is reproduced in Plate 135. (Actually there are thirteen *honji*, since both Fugen and Monju Bosatsu of the Ichi-man Jū-man are illus-

138. Nachi Falls. Colors on silk; ht 160 cm, w 60 cm. Kamakura period. Nezu Art Museum, Tokyo.

trated.) The three principal figures, surrounded by large double halos, have the serenity and dignity befitting such godly beings. One striking feature is the inclusion of a large image of an adherent of the Shugendō sect in the center foreground (Plate 136). Because there are numerous examples of scenes showing Emperor Goshirakawa, intimately associated with Kumano due to his many pilgrimages there, this figure of a typical pilgrim may well be the monk-emperor himself. According to historical records, pilgrims to Kumano wore white robes, hoods, silk undergarments, leggings, and straw sandals, and carried staffs. The portrayal of the monk-emperor's procession in the *Kumano Nachi Shrine Pilgrimage Mandala* (Plate 131) supports the assumption that this is the figure of the devout ruler.

Plate 137 is a Kumano *suijaku mandala* depicting the Shintō forms of all twelve *gongen* as well as a number of child deities. The principal deities are placed on something like a three-step doll shelf and are seated in rows on thick mats with striped borders. The goddess of Nachi, the god of the Shingū, and the priestly figure of the Hongū all sit before three-paneled screens. Because extant representations of the *suijaku* forms of these *kami* are rare, this painting and the Shintō sculptures still preserved in the three shrines (Plates 53 and 54) are of particular interest.

Both as a devotional image and as a landscape, the painting of Nachi Falls in Plate 138 is undoubtedly among the most remarkable works of art associated with the Kumano cult. Gleaming in the moonlight as as it cascades over a precipice, the fall occupies almost the full length of the *kakemono*. Around it are cypresses and jagged rocks depicted with marked realism and attention to detail. Although most shrine *mandalas*—for indeed, this work could be included in that category—are dominated by the wooden structures housing the gods, here only the roof of the shrine to the *kami* of the waterfall appears at the foot of the painting. This clearly suggests that the waterfall itself was regarded as the object of worship—and in fact, the religious impact of this simple landscape scene is strikingly like that of the more conventional *Amida Emerging from the Clouds* in Plate 126.

Although the source of inspiration for this work lies in a deep and ancient reverence for nature, its form of expression is extremely innovative. Believed to date from approximately 1300 (the same time as the *Ippen Shōnin Eden*), it was influenced by the Sung style that subsequently determined the direction of late Kamakura and Muromachi landscape painting. The use of space and brushwork here marked a turning point in the development of this genre in Japan.

Glossary

Amaterasu Omikami: sun goddess, central figure of the Shintō pantheon, and ancestress of the imperial family; enshrined in the Inner Sanctuary (Naikū) of the Ise Shrine

Amida Nyorai (Amitābha): deity who dwells in the Western Paradise of Sukhāvatī (Pure Land) and is believed to approach the earth to collect the soul of the deceased and carry it back to his realm, where it is reborn as a Buddha

aramitama: rough spirit of a deity, as opposed to his pacific spirit or *nigimitama* (*see*)

banshin: guardian deity, most commonly depicted in a group of thirty, one for each day of the month; their cult originated on Mount Hiei, inspired by Ennin

bosatsu (Bodhisattva): Buddhist saints devoted to the salvation of mankind; among the most popular are Monju, Jizō (*see*), and Kannon (*see*)

Chishō Daishi: ninth-century founder of the Mii-dera branch of the Tendai sect at the Mii-dera (Onjō-ji) temple at the foot of Mount Hiei

Dainichi Nyorai (Vairocana): central figure of the Esoteric Buddhist pantheon; divine essence of all other Buddhist deities and existence itself; equated with Amaterasu Omikami after the development of the *shimbutsu shūgō* movement (*see*)

Dengyō Daishi (Saichō): founder of the Tendai sect on Mount Hiei in the eighth century

dhāraṇī: Esoteric Buddhist magic formula or prayer

dōji: child deity or divine boy associated with the concept of youthfulness and rejuvenation of spiritual power

ema: votive picture; originally a portrayal of a horse, but later also the object of a devotee's prayers

Ennin: see Jikaku Daishi

En no Gyōja: seventh-century mountain hermit and miracle worker; legendary founder of the Shugen-dō sect (*see*)

gongen: incarnation of a Buddhist deity as a Shintō *kami* (*see*). With the development of *shimbutsu shūgō,* *kami* were believed to be alternate forms of Buddhist gods. (See also *suijaku.*)

goshintai: god-body, material object in which the divine soul resides

Hachiman: Shintō deity identified with Emperor Ojin and later considered a war god and the tutelary deity of the Minamoto clan. When depicted in the guise of a monk, he is referred to as Sōgyō Hachiman.

Hiei-zan: mountain center of the Tendai sect, whose principal temple is the Enryaku-ji; also the birthplace of the Sannō cult

-hiko: component of a Shintō deity's name meaning lord

-hime: component of a Shintō goddess's name meaning lady; for example, Tamayori-hime

honji-butsu (honji): original or fundamental form of a Buddhist god whose emanations as Shintō *kami* are called *suijaku* or *gongen*

honji-suijaku: see *shimbutsu-shūgō*

hōtō: treasure pagoda; circular building with a four-cornered roof with Buddhist affiliations

ichiboku-zukuri: single-woodblock construction; sculptural technique used in the early Heian period

Jikaku Daishi (Ennin): Tendai monk who visited China in the ninth century and wrote a diary describing his journey; introduced several Chinese deities to Japan

jingū-ji: Buddhist temple within the compound of a Shintō shrine

jinja: Shintō shrine without special rank

Jizō Bosatsu (Kṣitigarbha): one of many compassionate Bodhisattvas, guardian of travelers, women in childbirth, warriors, and children; generally shown in the guise of a monk with shaven head and staff

Jūichimen Kannon: eleven-headed Kannon

kakebotoke: round copper or wooden plaque on which Buddhist images are carved in relief

kami: Shintō deity; includes apotheosized human beings, heroes, and ancestors, as well as objects such as trees and mountains: anything possessed of superior power or an awe-inspiring nature

Kannon (Avalokiteśvara): Bodhisattva who serves as Amida's messenger and is devoted to helping man attain salvation; earthly dwelling is the mythical Mount Potalaka; can assume many forms

Kōbō Daishi (Kūkai): founder of the Shingon sect in Japan with Kōya-san as its monastic center and the Tō-ji in Kyoto as its other principal center; lived 774 to 835

koma-inu: lion-dog; creature resembling Pekinese dogs whose sculptures often guard the shrine entrance

Kōya-san: monastic center of the Shingon sect high in the mountains in Wakayama Prefecture

Kusanagi no Tsurugi: Grass-quelling Sword, part of the Imperial Regalia now enshrined in Atsuta Shrine, Nagoya

magatama: curved or comma-shaped jewel; the Yasakani no Magatama is part of the Imperial Regalia

mandala: painted or sculptural depiction of deities or their sanctuaries in a schematic form; commonly used to designate any image showing the relationships of Buddhist or Shintō deities

matsuri: Shintō festival

mi-are: a Shintō ceremony by which the *mitama* of a deity is rejuvenated

mikoshi (shin'yo): sacred palanquin used to transport the *kami* during festivals

-mikoto: component of a Shintō deity's name meaning august one

mishotai: mirrors, often inscribed with images, used as objects of worship

mitama: soul or spirit of a deity (see also *nigimitama* and *aramitama*)

miya: shrine, equivalent of *jinja*

naishi dokoro: see Yata no Kagami

nigimitama: pacific spirit of a deity as opposed to his rough spirit or *aramitama*

Nyoirin Kannon (Cintāmaṇicakra Avalokiteśvara): form of Kannon holding a magic jewel *(nyoirin)* in the right hand; *honji* of Seiryū Gongen

raigō-zu: image of Amida descending from heaven with his retinue to receive the believer's soul

shaden shintō: shrine Shintō; designates the post-Nara phase in which the shrine structure rather than natural sites played a prominent role

shaku: flat, elongated wooden scepter; symbol of dignity and authority

Senju Kannon (Sahasrabhuja Avalokiteśvara): thousand-armed Kannon

shikinen sengū: periodic rebuilding of the principal sanctuary of a shrine and renewal of all its furnishings and treasures

shimbutsu-shūgō: fusion of gods and Buddhas, theory according to which Buddhist gods are original forms *(honji)* and Shintō deities their incarnations *(suijaku* or *gongen);* also called the *honji-suijaku* theory

shimpō: divine treasure; article offered for the use of the *kami,* including furnishings, clothing, and arms *shintai-zan:* sacred mountain thought to be a divine being

shizen shintō: natural Shintō; designates the pre-Nara phase in which nature worship in sacred sites predominated

Shugendō: sect of wandering ascetics with Tendai and Shingon affiliations founded by En no Gyōja; adherents are called *yamabushi*

Siddham script: variant of the Indian *Devanagari* script used to write Sanskrit

suijaku: trace, manifestation, or incarnation; *kami* viewed as the emanation of the Buddhist god who is his *honji* (see also *gongen*)

Takamagahara: Heavenly Plain; abode of Amaterasu Omikami and numerous other deities

ujigami: tutelary or special guardian deity of a clan or locality

wakamiya: subsidiary sanctuary often enshrining children of the principal deity; also designates the youthful form of a *kami*

yamabushi: "those who sleep in the mountains"; mountain-climbing ascetics, adherents of the Shugendō sect

Yata no Kagami: eight-petaled mirror given to Ninigi no Mikoto by Amaterasu Omikami when he descended to rule the earth; enshrined in Ise Shrine as the embodiment of the *mitama* of the sun goddess; also called *naishi dokoro*

yosegi-zukuri: joined-woodblock construction; sculpture technique used especially from the later Heian period

Zaō Gongen: tutelary deity of Mount Kimpu and special guardian of the Shugendō sect

Bibliography

General

Basic Terms of Shintō. Shintō Committee for the IXth International Congress for the History of Religions. Tokyo: Kokugakuin University, 1958.

Jinja (Shintō Shrines) and Festivals. Jinja Honchō (The Association of Shintō Shrines). March 1970.

Literature

Aston, William G. (tr.): *Nihongi: Chronicles of Japan from the Earliest Times to A.D. 697*, 2 vols. London: Allen and Unwin, 1956.

Bock, Felicia G. (tr.): *Engi-shiki: Procedures of the Engi Era (901–922)*, Books I–V. Tokyo: Sophia University, 1970.

Philippi, Donald L. (tr.): *Kojiki*. Princeton, N. J.: Princeton University Press, 1969.

Sadler, A. L. (tr.): *Saka's Diary of a Pilgrim to Ise (Ise Dai-jinja Sankeiki)*. Tokyo: Meiji Society, 1940.

Waley, Arthur (tr.): *The Tale of Genji: A Novel in Six Parts by Lady Murasaki*. Tokyo: Tuttle, 1970.

Religion

Herbert, Jean: *Shintō, the Fountainhead of Japan*. New York: Stein and Day, 1967.

Holtom, D. C.: *The National Faith of Japan: A Study in Modern Shintō*. New York: Paragon Reprint, 1965.

Hori, Ichirō: *Folk Religion in Japan—Continuity and Change*. Tokyo: University of Tokyo Press, 1968.

Kidder, J. E.: *Japan Before Buddhism*. London: Thames and Hudson, 1966.

Matsunaga, Alicia: *The Buddhist Theory of Assimilation: The Historical Development of the Honji-Suijaku Theory*. Tokyo: Sophia University and Tuttle, 1969.

Ono, S.: *Shintō, the Kami Way*. Tokyo: Bridgeway Press, 1962.

Ponsonby-Fane, R.: *Studies in Shintō and Shrines*. Kyoto: Ponsonby Memorial Society, 1962.

———: *The Vicissitudes of Shintō*. Kyoto: Ponsonby Memorial Society, 1963.

———: *Visiting Famous Shrines in Japan*. Kyoto: Ponsonby Memorial Society, 1964.

Shintō Art and Architecture

Akiyama, Aisaburō: *Shintō and Its Architecture*. Kyoto: Japan Welcome Society, 1936.

Kidder, J. E.: *The Birth of Japanese Art*. London: Allen and Unwin, 1965.

Nagai, Shin'ichi: *The Gods of Kumano*. Tokyo: Kodansha, 1969.

Tange, Kenzo, and Noboru Kawazoe: *Ise, Prototype of Japanese Architecture*. Cambridge, Mass.: M.I.T. Press, 1965.

Articles

Anderson, Suzanne: "Legends of Holy Men of Early Japan," *Monumenta Serica*, XXVII (1969), 258–320.

Blacker, Carmen: "The Divine Boy in Japanese Buddhism," *Asian Folklore Studies*, XII (1963), 77–88.

Holtom, D. C.: "Japanese Votive Pictures: The Ikoma Ema," *Monumenta Nipponica*, 1938.

Index

The Arts of Japan Series

These books, which are a selection from the larger series on the arts of Japan published in Japanese by the Shibundō Publishing Company of Tokyo, will in future volumes deal with such topics as haniwa, ink painting, architecture, furniture, lacquer, ceramics, textiles, masks, Buddhist painting and sculpture, and early Western-style prints.

Published:

In preparation:

The "weathermark" identifies this English-language edition as having been planned, designed, and produced at the Tokyo offices of John Weatherhill, Inc., in collaboration with Shibundō Publishing Company. Book design and typography by Dana Levy. Text composed by Kenkyūsha. Engraving by Hanshichi. Printing by Nissha and Hanshichi. Bound at Oguchi Binderies. The type of the main text is set in 11-pt. Bembo with hand-set Goudy Bold for display.